The Hopeless Church of Little Faith!

(The Unholy Church of Graceful Sinners, who are Mostly just Liars and Hypocrites!)

By
The Good Pastor of Uncommon Sense!

Book 121 ♥

(The Cover Photo shows a Brazilian Agate with all-Natural Colors!)

Copyright, Dedication and Introduction

By the Honest Observer and Chief Agitator!

ISBN — 979-8657-7506-69

00-01 [_] This Inspired Book is COPYRIGHTED 2020 ADR (After Death and Resurrection) by "The Worldwide People's Revolution!" (A Comprehensive Plan for Obtaining Worldwide Law, Order, Obedience, Peace and True Prosperity!) By The Worldwide People's Revolution!® Book 108. All Rights are Reserved for the Truth's Sake. No Portion of this Exceptionally Good Book (♥) shall be Reproduced by any Means for Sale without Written Permission from **The Worldwide People's Revolution!®** However, with our Permission, anyone in the Whole World may Reproduce Exact Copies, and Sell them for a Reasonable Profit, and Keep 90% of the Net Profits for their own Prosperity: beCause our Selected King only Wants 10 percent of the Net Profits for the Construction of: **"The Great World TEMPLE of PEACE!"** (The Glory of Jerusalem Arises Again in the Great State of Flexible Texas!) By The Worldwide People's Revolution!® Book 017B, which will be Located in the Center of: **"A New Jerusalem in the Great State of Flexible Texas!"** (HOW to make Good Use of the Mississippi River!) By The Worldwide People's Revolution!® Book 090, which Temple will be the Headquarters for: **"The New RIGHTEOUS One-World Government!"** (HOW to Establish a Righteous One-World Government without Going to WAR!) By The Worldwide People's Revolution!® Book 056: beCause there are no less than **"101 Good Reasons and Great Advantages for Establishing a Righteous One-World Government!"** (Government By the People, Of the People, and For the People!) By The Worldwide People's Revolution!® B-104.

00-02 [_] O Honest Observer and Chief Agitator, suppose that we do not Believe in a Wicked One-World Government, what should we do with our 10% of the Net Profits from the Sales of this Uninspired Book, which Capitalizes far too many Words, which is Contrary to our Vain Traditions? Indeed, I Refuse to Study: "Justifications for Capitalizations!" (WHY our Selected King DEFIES the School of FOOLS by Capitalizing LOVE and HATE!) By The Worldwide People's Revolution!® Book 049: beCause, I am Fully Persuaded with King Agrippa that your much Learning has Driven thee Totally Insane with the Apostle Paul, who was Tempted by Satan to Capitalize *the Light of the World;* but, he did not Yield to the Temptation, nor should I. †§‡§§

00-03 [_] Well, my Poor Deceived Friend, or Potential Enemy, if that is how you Honestly Feel about it, be Sure to put a Large RED-X Mark in the Box for Verse 00-01: beCause of Disagreeing with the Statement; and put a Large GREEN-X Mark in Verse 00-02, which Indicates that you Agree with Verse 00-02, and that you Disagree with Verse 00-01. Otherwise, we will all Know that you are the Person who has been Driven Totally Insane by your IGNORANCE, being like the Trumpeter and his Crazy Followers, who showed up at the Trump/Pence Campaign Rally in Tulsa, Brokelahoma, during the Pandemic, with the Hope that they were Immune to any Bugs. The Wise People just Stayed at Home, and did not take any Unnecessary Chances: beCause they already knew in advance that President Trump would not Reveal any Truths that might Liberate them from any Sicknesses nor Diseases, being one of the most Ignorant Persons on the Good Earth, even though he took Precautions to Avoid Shaking Hands, Kissing and Hugging his Supporters. †§‡§§

00-04 [_] The Colorful little Rocks in the Picture on the previous Page are Representative of Various Kinds of People, who are Congregated in the same Church, who come in Various Sizes, Shapes, Colors, and Races, who are Pretending to be at One with God, who Falsely Teach that *"... all men were created equal,"* when they all Know for a Fact that no one was Created Equal with anyone else in any Way: beCause, each Person is Unique and Special, even if they are Unaware of it. Moreover, as for them having Equal Rights with Moses, Samuel, Elijah and King Jesus Christ, we will all Discover during the Day of Judgment that *Numbers 16* was not Written in Vain.‡

00-05 [_] O Honest Observer and Chief Agitator, are you Suggesting that Saint Thomas Jefferson had it all WRong? Is it not Self-evident that all Men were Created with Equal Tally Whackers and Chime Bells, who Sire Children who are also Equal with Jesus Christ and Saint Paul? Surely, you have gotten your Head Screwed on Backwards, somehow; or, even Upside Down. Have you not been Watching the "Black Lives Matter" Protests? Therefore, this Inspired Book is now DEDICATED to them! {See: "Is America a White Nation with a Black Heart?" (How to Separate Truth from Fiction!) By The Good Pastor of Uncommon Sense! Book 118.} †§‡§§

00-06 [_] Well, my Friend, it was those Protests that Inspired the Good Pastor of Uncommon Sense to Write this Inspired Book. Therefore, I Hope that you "Reed" it with an Open, Honest Mind. †§‡

00-07 [_] O Honest Observer and Chief Agitator, which False Church of Little Faith does your Selected King Belong to? Or, is he an Atheist? I used to be an Atheist, until I Met Jesus on the Road to Damascus, you might say, when I got Converted by the Bright Light of Provable Truths!

00-08 [_] Well, my Friend, I can Assure you that our Selected King is NOT an Atheist, nor an Unbeliever; but, he has more Faith than a thousand Men, put Together, which is made known by the Fact that he has Written more Inspired Books than any Person who ever Lived, which is likely to be the World Record for all Ages to Come: beCause his Inspired Books preezent those "Guaranteed Solutions!" (HOW to Solve our Local and Global Problems in the Most-Rational Manner Possible!) By The Worldwide People's Revolution!® Book 080, which no other Author has ever Presented. In Fact, you could read all of the Books by Mark Twain, for Example, and not Discover so much as one Guaranteed Solution for anything! However, his Books are Entertaining and Fascinating to read. Indeed, they might even be more

Interesting than the Colorful Books by our Selected King, unless you might be Looking for those Guaranteed Solutions, in which Case, no one can begin to Compete with our Selected King: beCause his Solutions come from GOD. For Example, those **"GLORIOUS Swanky Hotels Castles and Fortresses!" (Beautiful Planned City States for WISE Intelligent Well-Educated People with Common Sense and Good Understanding!) By The Worldwide People's Revolution!® Book** 019B, have more than 5,000 Good Reasons and Great Advantages for Building them, with ZERO Great Disadvantages for Righteous People, which nothing else in this World of Wonders has! †§‡

00-09 [_] O Honest Observer and Chief Agitator, I must Confess that Provable Truths Flow Out of the Amazing Heart of your Selected King, like Sparkling Spring Water from Mount Everest, in a Never-ending Flow of Refreshing Living Water, as Jesus Christ might say to his Blest Disciples.

00-10 [_] Well, my Friend, that is beCause our Selected King has the Holy Spirit to Guide him, who is Miles Ahead of everyone else; or, should I say: Centuries Ahead of everyone else? Indeed, when all other Plans for Worldwide Law, Order, Obedience, Peace and True Prosperity have been Exhausted, the Swanky Fortress System will Prove to be the Best Solution: beCause it is God's Solution, which has no Faults, at all! In Fact, I Challenge you to Discover any Faults with it, at all.

This is the MENU on the Table of Contents
for a Satisfying Feast of Provable Truths!

{HEADNOTE: This Inspired Book contains a few Photographs with Explanations, plus about 27,000 Special Words for the Unholy Church of Graceful Sinners, who are probably Sick and Tired of being Liars and Hypocritters, or Hypo-Critics for that Matter, who Condemn themselves!}

{Missing Chapters will be Supplied, if they are Needed for Better Understanding.}

FOOTNOTE: For Explanations of Symbols (†§‡§§), see: "Which Church is the Right Church?" (Can all Churches be Correct?) **By The Good Pastor of Uncommon Sense!** Book 119.

ATTENTION: If you find certain Words that are too Small to read with Comfort, without any Strain on your Eyes, we Recommend that you read the 8.5- by 11-inch Colored Edition, which is also less Expensive than the 6- by 9-inch Colored Edition: beCause of having less Sheets of Paper. That Edition will also have Larger Pictures and Clearer Drawings. But, of course, the E-Book Edition is the least Expensive, if you are Extremely Poor, and need to Save as much Money as Possible; and Multitudes of People are now Extremely Poor: beCause of not being set up Properly at Home for Living a Good Life, who have no All-Mineral Organic Gardens to Feed themselves, as they should have, and would have, if our Selected King were in Charge of Things. Therefore, you could say that, "DUMBmocracy is getting its Just Reward for Rejecting Provable Truths." Nevertheless, this Inspired Book Explains HOW to Overcome that Problem, and get everyone Set Up Properly for Living and Working at Home.

— Chapter 01 —

Why is it called a Hopeless Church?

01-01 [_] {HEADNOTE: After writing the Previous Book, called: "Do People Go to Heaven when they Die?" (The Unbelievable Truth about Life and Death!) **By The Good Pastor of Uncommon Sense!** Book 120, I just Happened to be Watching the Evening News on YouTube, and the following YouTube Program came on after the News, which Confirmed what I was saying in the above Book: https://youtu.be/T3YeonnAXyU — Top 50 Puzzling Ancient Ruins that Scientists, Archaeologists and Historians are still Debating. End of Headnote. Beginning of Liit.}

01-02 [_] Of course, there is always HOPE that any Group of People, including the Edomites and Trumpites, might *"See the Light,"* as Hank Williams might say, and thus, not be so Hopeless; but, in this Case, I am only Referring to those People who are Actually HOPELESS, who have Refused to Study any Books that might Prove their False Beliefs to be WRong, according to their own *Holy Bibles,* which come in more than 200 Different Translations, which is Proof that People Discovered Mistranslations, and Decided to TRY to Correct those "Mistakes," and thus, they Produced more Translations: beCause they Obviously did not Discover *The New MAGNIFIED Version of the Scriptures,* which is NOT a Translation of any Kind; but, it is an Inspired Version by the Holy Spirit, which makes it far more Accurate: beCause the Holy Spirit did not Die, nor even go to Sleep; but, she is still Doing her Good Work, which is to Inspire People to Write Truths, even if they are Atheists and Agnostics, who also have a Right to have their own Honest Opinions.

01-03 [_] O Good Pastor of Uncommon Sense, it is written that *"Prophecies in Ancient Times did not come by the Will of Sinful Men; but, Holy Men, who were Inspired by God, Wrote the Scriptures as they were Moved by the Holy Spirit," — Second Peter 1:21,* which is not the Case for a Novelist, who is Inspired by Satan, who usually writes Nonsense and Dialog — such as, *The Adventures of Tom Sawyer,* or *The Adventures of Huckleberry Finn,* by Master Mark Twain, who was a Literary Genius and Humorist, who is still America's Premier Author, when it comes to Reason and Logic, who was one of the few People who could THINK and Remember Well, while you are Basically just a DUNCE, as Mark Twain might say: beCause you still Vainly Imagine that there is some Hope for these False Churches, which have Rejected

Biblical Truths, and have Invented their own False Doctrines of the Devil — such as that Fake Ownership Doctrine, whereby they have made themselves into Education Slaves, just to get their Deplorable Diplomas, whereby they might obtain so-called "good jobs," whereby they might be made into Work Slaves, Tax Slaves, Insurance Slaves, Rent Slaves, Home-owner Slaves, Interest Slaves, Mortgage Bills Slaves, Credit Card Debt Bills Slaves, ElecTrickery Bills Slaves, Food Bills Slaves, Water Bills Slaves, Gas Bills Slaves, Transportation Bills Slaves, Repair Bills Slaves, Telephone Bills Slaves, Entertainment Bills Slaves, Drug Bills Slaves, Doctor Bills Slaves, Hospital Bills Slaves, Childcare Bills Slaves, Nursery Home Bills Slaves, and all of those other Kinds of SLAVES that are only Mentioned in: "Modern Deceived SLAVES!" (10 Simple Steps for Liberating ALL Modern Slaves, Worldwide, Including Yourself!) **By** Liberty and Justice for ALL! Book 113. Read it. †§‡§§

01-04 [_] Well, my Friend, most American Republicans, Democrats and Independent Jackasses have Bought into the False Ownership Doctrine of the Devil, which they say is BIBLICAL: beCause Father Abraham was a Rich Man with much Silver and Gold, as well as Sheeps, Goats, Camels, Asses, Horses, and Cattles of all Kinds, who had more than 500 Voluntary Servants, who Helped him to Attend to all of those Creatures: beCause Abraham was the Leader of that Ancient Tribe of Israelite Warmongers, who was also a Man of WAR, according to *Genesis 14:14,* which is no Secret; but, Jesus Christ was a Pacifist, who Turned the other Cheek, who Believed in doing Good to those People who did Evil to him, just to Heap Up HOT COALS of Fire on their Heads, as the Apostle Paul put it in *Romans 12:20,* who was also a Pacifist, who Firmly Believed in: "The Swanky Sword of Divine Truths!" (The Most-Powerful Weapon in the Whole Universe!) By The Worldwide People's Revolution!® Book 067: beCause, only the Truth can Win in the End.

01-05 [_] O Good Pastor of Uncommon Sense, it seems like the *Old Testament* God had a Totally Different Personality, than the *New Testament* God, as if he had Learned a lot about Mankind during those thousands of Years, and Decided that it was Best if the Romans should Govern this World, in spite of their Cruelties and Slavery Systems, which was Confirmed by the Apostle Paul in *Romans 13,* which goes into Great Details to Explain that every Soul should be in Subjection to the Highest Powers: beCause, *"... there is no Power that is not Ordained by God,"* which is to say that God Ordained Adolf Hitler to make War against the Jews, whereby 16 Million of them Died in Concentration Work Camps, which we call the Jewish Holocaust, whereby only a few thousand Jews

Survived it, who Immediately went into the Production of Making Babies, whereby they Produced no less than 15 Million Babies between 1945 and 1950, whereby the World Almanac could read Correctly about the World CENSUS, which, in 1940, Reported that there were 19.5 Million Jews in the Whole World; and then, in 1950, they Reported that there were 17.5 Million Jews in the Whole World. Therefore, if 16 Million Jews were Killed during the NAZI Holocaust, that would have left only 3.5 Million Jews in the Whole World, half of whom would have been Women, and half of them would have been too Young or too Old to Bear any Children, which Means that only 0.875 Million Womb-men gave Birth to about 14 Million Babies in only 4 Years: beCause the Census was taken in 1949! Yes, it is just Astounding Information to Think about it, if you can do your Mathematics Correctly, even if only 6 Million Jews were Killed or Died from Sicknesses, Diseases or Old Age during the HoloHOAX: beCause, on Average, Jews have Historically Produced only 1.3 Children per Family, which Means that those Surviving Jews might have Produced a Million Babies from 1945 to 1949, at most, which is a very Long Ways from 14 Million. Nevertheless, you are Welcome to Believe whatever Jewish Lies that you Like. †§‡§§

01-06 [_] Well, my Potential Friend or Enemy, I Seriously Doubt that the God of LOVE Ordained Adolf Hitler to Murder his "Chosen People," nor the 40,000,000 White Christian Russians that Saint Joseph Stalin had Executed in one Way or another during his Reign of Communist TERROR, which was Overlooked by the Federal Government of: "The Divided States of United Lies!" (The so-called "United States of North America" in Disguise!) By The Worldwide People's Revolution!® Book 058, which Required the History Channel another 40 Years for them to Confess the Goodness of Saint Joseph Stalin, if you know what I Mean, seeing that I am being very Sarcastic, which is WHY all such Statements are followed by Section Symbols (§§), which Means that I am being very Funny, even though there is Absolutely nothing Funny about 60 Million People Dying in a Hateful War that could have easily been Prevented, just by Yielding to: "The Swanky Sword of Divine Truths!" (The Most-Powerful Weapon in the Whole Universe!) By The Worldwide People's Revolution!® Book 067, by Calling for: "The GREAT Worldwide TELEVISED Court HEARING!" (That Great Meeting of the Most-Intelligent and Well-Educated Minds!) By The Worldwide People's Revolution!® Book 041B, except that they did not have Televisions in 1939, when Honest Adolf Hitler called for the Leaders of Great Britain, France, the Union of Soviet Socialist Republicans, and United States of North America to Hold an International RADIO DEBATE, in Order to Inform the Electors about the Situation in Germany, whereby the Electors might Decide WHO is Telling the TRUTH, and WHO is Lying to them, which turned out to be those Lying Conniving EDOMITES, who WON World War 2: beCause they Gained a couple Trillion Dollars by it, while the Russians Lost about 22 Million Young Men for nothing, and the British People and Americans Lost several Million, while Millions of others Deserted their Armies: beCause they had no Longing Desires to Sacrifice their Lives for the Sake of Enriching RICH Jewish Bankers on both Sides of the War! But, of course, that Bad News was never Reported by the Snooze Reporters. Indeed, … (Check the Appropriate Boxes that you Agree with, or Disagree with, using the Correct Color Code.)

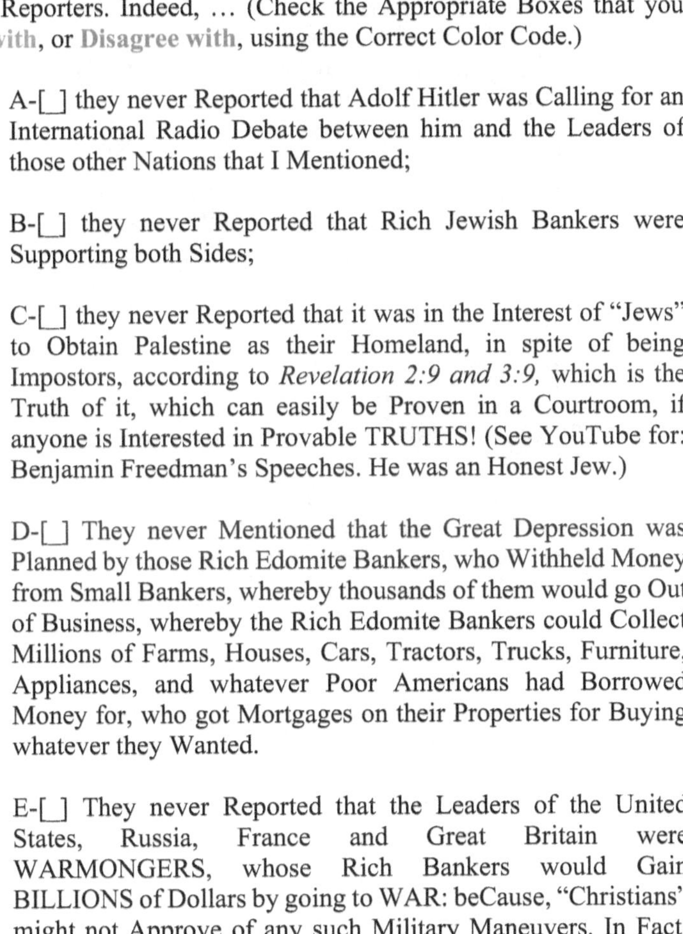

A-[ ] they never Reported that Adolf Hitler was Calling for an International Radio Debate between him and the Leaders of those other Nations that I Mentioned;

B-[ ] they never Reported that Rich Jewish Bankers were Supporting both Sides;

C-[ ] they never Reported that it was in the Interest of "Jews" to Obtain Palestine as their Homeland, in spite of being Impostors, according to *Revelation 2:9 and 3:9,* which is the Truth of it, which can easily be Proven in a Courtroom, if anyone is Interested in Provable TRUTHS! (See YouTube for: Benjamin Freedman's Speeches. He was an Honest Jew.)

D-[ ] They never Mentioned that the Great Depression was Planned by those Rich Edomite Bankers, who Withheld Money from Small Bankers, whereby thousands of them would go Out of Business, whereby the Rich Edomite Bankers could Collect Millions of Farms, Houses, Cars, Tractors, Trucks, Furniture, Appliances, and whatever Poor Americans had Borrowed Money for, who got Mortgages on their Properties for Buying whatever they Wanted.

E-[ ] They never Reported that the Leaders of the United States, Russia, France and Great Britain were WARMONGERS, whose Rich Bankers would Gain BILLIONS of Dollars by going to WAR: beCause, "Christians" might not Approve of any such Military Maneuvers. In Fact, not even Atheists would Approve of it, if they had Children, who might get Murdered during such Hateful Wars.

F-[_] The Jewish-controlled News Media did not Advertise one Word of Truth about the German National Socialist Worker's Party, under the Administration of that Wicked, WICKED Adolf Hitler, who got the Germans OUT of the Great Depression within only 6 Months, after he got into Total Control, while the Europeans and Americans went right on Suffering with the Great Depression for another 10 Years: beCause, they did not Accept the Economic Policies of that Wicked, WICKED Adolf Hitler, who was Determined to put those Lying Conniving Edomites OUT of Business: beCause they Caused the Great Depression, as well as World Wars 1 and 2, which has been Explained in several Good Books, if anyone is Interested in Learning anything about what Actually Happened, which only about 0.001% of the General Population is Interested in: beCause most People only Want to LIV, while Paying their Endless Bills: beCause they LOVE those Edomite Bills! Otherwise, they would "VOTE for The GOAT!" (The New Political Party that has Guaranteed Solutions for our Massive Problems!) By The Worldwide People's Revolution!® Book 109, and be DONE with all Bills! †§‡

G-[_] The Lying Conniving Edomites never Reported anything about "The New RIGHTEOUS One-World Government!" (HOW to Establish a Righteous One-World Government without Going to WAR!) By The Worldwide People's Revolution!® Book 056, in spite of the Fact that there are more than "101 Good Reasons and Great Advantages for Establishing a Righteous One-World Government!" (Government By the People, Of the People, and For the People!) By The Worldwide People's Revolution!® Book 104, even as there are more than 5,000 Good Reasons and Great Advantages for Building those: "GLORIOUS Swanky Hotels Castles and Fortresses!" (Beautiful Planned City States for WISE Intelligent Well-Educated People with Common Sense and Good Understanding!) By The Worldwide People's Revolution!® Book 019B, which is Proven in: "The Right Design for Living!" (A List of Great Advantages for Building Beautiful Planned City States!) By The Worldwide People's Revolution!® Book 012B, which is a Companion Book of: "The Low Court of Supreme Injustices is Brought to Trial!" (Our Selected King Butts Heads with the United States Supreme Court, with or without their Black Robes of Hypocrisies and Lies!) By The Worldwide People's

Revolution!® Book 011B, which those Wicked Politicians Refuze to REED: beCause they are Graduates of "The Public School of IGNERUNT FQLZ!" (HOW we have been GRAATLEE DISEEVD by Capitalism!) By The Worldwide People's Revolution!® Book 024B, which is still spelling NOLIJ like the Barbarians, as in: K-N-O-W-L-E-D-G-E, instead of N-O-L-I-J: beCause they Suffer with Chronic Constipation of their Minds, whereby they cannot Think nor Remember! †§‡

H-[_] The Edomites did not Advertise "The LUSCIOUS All-Mineral Organic Method of Gardening!" (HOW to Grow DELICIOUS Satisfying Foods for Potential Kingz and Kweenz in Beautiful Swanky PALACES!) By The Worldwide People's Revolution!® Book 021B, which is a Companion Book of: "Orgimmick Gardening at its Best!" (HOW to Grow Delicious Satisfying Foods without a 10 Million-Dollar Investment!) By The Worldwide People's Revolution!® Book 079: beCause, someone might Discover that they can Dig Up enough Potatoes during 4 Hours, using a Potato Digging Fork, to Feed themselves and their Family all Year, IF they Liv on the Land, and have a GARDEN to Feed themselves from! †§‡

I-[__] In Fact, they could Gather up enough Butternut Squashes to Feed themselves all Winter, in just 2 Hours, if they were all Set Up Properly for LIVING! But, the Edomites never Mention that in: "The Public School of IGNERUNT FQLZ!" (HOW we have been GRAATLEE DISEEVD by Capitalism!) By The Worldwide People's Revolution!® Book 024B: beCause that would not be very Profitable for those Gross Edomite Grocery Stores, which are Relying on IGNORANCE among the Masses of "Modern Deceived SLAVES!" (10 Simple Steps for Liberating ALL Modern Slaves, Worldwide, Including Yourself!) **By Liberty and Justice for ALL!** Book 113, who have never Studied: "Are you a Jobless Graduate of the SKQL uv FQLZ?" (HOW to Get a GOUD EJUKAASHUN without Robbing the Bank!) By The Worldwide People's Revolution!® Book 020B, which is a Companion Book of: **"Poverty Hunger Riots Strikes Police Brutalities Election Deceptions and Civil Wars!" (The High Price that we Earthlings have Paid for Leaving the Good Land!) By The Worldwide People's Revolution!®** Book 014B. Indeed, they Falsely Claim to be EDUCATED, just beCause of having Edomite Diplomas; but, a True Education would at least know how to Feed itself.

J-[__] Those Lying Conniving Edomites have never Mentioned: **"Seven Great Armies of Working Soldiers!" (HOW to Provide a Way for Everyone to WORK: so as to Eliminate Poverty, Crimes, Drug Abuses, Prisons and Unnecessary Taxes!) By The Worldwide People's Revolution!®** Book 015B, who are Hired, According to: "A List of FAIR Swanky Wages!" (The Equitable Wage System!) By The Worldwide

People's Revolution!® Book 065, in Order to Build those: "Beautiful Swanky PALACES!" (A New Concept in Living Habits — Swanky Palaces for Poor People!) By The Worldwide People's Revolution!® Book 066: beCause, if everyone in the World is Living within a Swanky PALACE, why would anyone Want to go to WAR? Indeed, they only Want True JUSTICE, not any Hateful Bloody Gory WARS! Therefore, they should be the First to DEMAND: "The GREAT Worldwide TELEVISED Court HEARING!" (That Great Meeting of the Most-Intelligent and Well-Educated Minds!) By The Worldwide People's Revolution!® Book 041B. However, the Edomite Snooze Reporters have never Mentioned it! For Example, have you ever Heard about it, until NOW? †§‡§§

K-[_] Kindhearted King Jesus would not be Organizing "The Swanky Associations of Working Soldiers!" (A Fascinating Collection of Various Kinds of Voluntary Working Soldiers!) By The Worldwide People's Revolution!® Book 018B, whereby they might Feed themselves at those: "Royal Swanky Buffets!" (The Best Feasts in the Whole World!) By The Worldwide People's Revolution!® Book 103, by "The LUSCIOUS All-Mineral Organic Method of Gardening!" (HOW to Grow DELICIOUS Satisfying Foods for Potential Kingz and Kweenz in Beautiful Swanky PALACES!) By The Worldwide People's Revolution!® Book 021B, if he were in Charge of Things on this Good Earth: beCause, he has been Listening to "The PRAYERS of PUMPKINHEADS!" (This Book is otherwise known as the Prayers of Preachers, Priests, Professors, Politicians, Prostitutes, Policemen, Pumpkinheads, Punks, Prisoners, and other Professionals — in other Words, the Capital P People!) By The Worldwide People's Revolution!® Book 007B, who have never "red" "All of the Arguments are in Favor of our Selected King, who has Zero Challengers!" (Before you Attend another Election Deception, you should Carefully Study this Inspired Book with an Honest Open Mind!) By The Worldwide People's Revolution!® Book 085, much less: "How all Women can Get True Justice without Getting Divorced from God!" (The Unjust Case of Judge Brett Kavanaugh and Doctor Christine Blasey Ford is now Revisited by a Wise Son of King Solomon!) By The Worldwide People's Revolution!® Book 087, which is a

Companion Book of: "HOW to Make America (and all other Nations) Really GREAT Without Telling any LIES!" (The Founding Fathers would have Loved it!) By The Worldwide People's Revolution!® Book 092. †§‡§§

L-[_] Lots of Laughs! Kindhearted King Jesus is nothing but a "Christian" MYTH, which was Invented by those Lying Conniving Edomites to SELL BOOKS: beCause that is the one Thing that they are Really GOOD at, which is WHY that they are Advertising all of the Inspired Books by: "The Worldwide People's Revolution!" (A Comprehensive Plan for Obtaining Worldwide Law, Order, Obedience, Peace and True Prosperity!) By The Worldwide People's Revolution!® Book 108. Indeed, they run at least 6 Advertisements, each Hour, on Televisions and Radios: beCause they have no less than 120 Books to SELL, whereby Amazon can Profit by no less than 20 Trillion Dollars, if they Play their Cards Correctly: beCause, each Book comes in 3 to 5 Different Editions, including Leather-bound Hand-carved Editions: beCause they are the Best Books in the Whole World, which alone are Worthy of such Beautiful Covers: beCause of being "An Amazing Collection of Wit and Wisdom!" (The Marvelous Tale of the Colorful Peacock from Angel Ridge, and the Strong Rope of Everlasting Hope!) By The Worldwide People's Revolution!® Book 048.

M-[ ] "For the Love of Money!" (The Strange Things that People Say and Do to Get more Money!) By The Worldwide People's Revolution!® Book 003B, is "The Root Cause for almost all Evils!" (The Strange Things that People Say and Do to Get more Money!) By The Worldwide People's Revolution!® Book 078: beCause that is "The Nature of CAPITALISM!" (A List of the EVILS of CAPITALISM!) By The Worldwide People's Revolution!® Book 038; but, it is NOT the MOTIVE for "LIGHTNING STRIKES Versus Lightning Bugs!" (HOW you can Become Moderately RICH, without Telling any Lies nor Selling any Trash!) By The Worldwide People's Revolution!® Book 074: beCause that would Contradict "The Seven Basic Spiritual Building Blocks of LIFE!" (Faith Hope Trust Love Patience Persistence and Obedience!) By The Worldwide People's Revolution!® Book 036, which is what Motivates our Selected King, whose Primary Interest is "The GREAT Worldwide TELEVISED Court HEARING!" (That Great Meeting of the Most-Intelligent and Well-Educated Minds!) By The Worldwide People's Revolution!® Book 041B, which should also be the Primary Interest of the News Media; but, behold, they have never Mentioned it: beCause they are Obviously NOT SEEKING "Provable Truths that True Christians cannot Rightly Deny!" (A Fair Challenge for all Professing "Christians" to Meditate on with Honest Open Minds!) By The Worldwide People's Revolution!® Book 086, much less: "Beautiful Swanky Stone Dome Home COMPLEXES!" (HOW to Build SECURE Tax-proof, Insurance-proof, Self-air-conditioned, Paint-proof, Rot-proof, Termite-proof, Mouse-proof, Fireproof, Tornado-proof, Hurricane-proof, Thief-proof, and BOMB-PROOF Houses!) By The Worldwide People's Revolution!® Book 102, for everyone in the Whole World, whereby "Poverty Hunger Riots Strikes Police Brutalities Election Deceptions and Civil Wars!" (The High Price that we Earthlings have Paid for Leaving the Good Land!) By The Worldwide People's Revolution!® Book 014B, might CEASE: beCause of Living in PEACE!

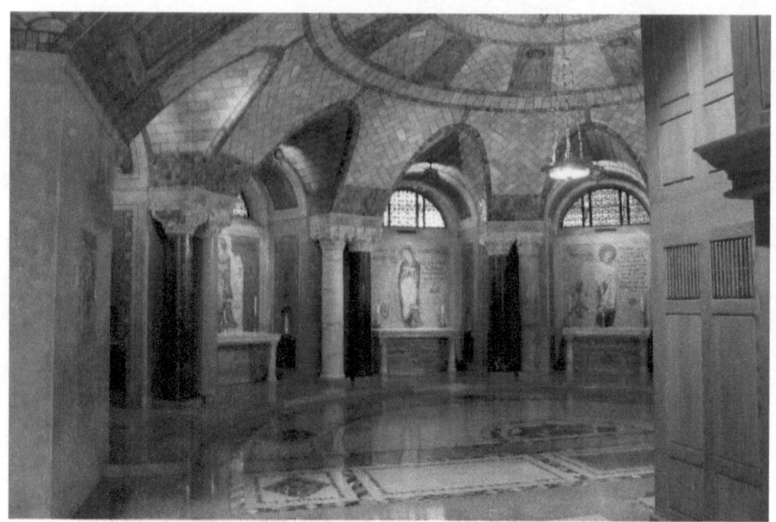

N-[_] Indeed, those Fake News Reporters would say, Not everyone could Afford to Build nor Buy such "Beautiful Swanky Stone Dome Home COMPLEXES!" (HOW to Build SECURE Tax-proof, Insurance-proof, Self-air-conditioned, Paint-proof, Rot-proof, Termite-proof, Mouse-proof, Fireproof, Tornado-proof, Hurricane-proof, Thief-proof, and BOMB-PROOF Houses!) By The Worldwide People's Revolution!® Book 102, which have Polished Marble Walls and Polished Granite Floors, which might Cost a Billion Dollars for just one COMPLEX! After all, the Shrine of Immaculate Conceptions Costed 4 Billion Dollars, which would now Cost 32 Billion. Therefore, HOW could anyone Afford to Liv in such Fine Mansions? However, that is only beCause of Accepting that FALSE Ownership Doctrine as a Good Thing, when it is the Most Evil Thing that those Wicked GREEDY SELFISH Edomites Invented, which we can now put into the Capitalist Trash Can, along with all other False Doctrines, which can be Proven at: "The GREAT Worldwide TELEVISED Court HEARING!" (That Great Meeting of the Most-Intelligent and Well-Educated Minds!) By The Worldwide People's Revolution!® Book 041B!

O-[_] Are there no Options to Choose from? Must we all be FORCED to Eat those Sweet Fragrant DELICIOUS Organic Mangos? Indeed, I Love my Tax Slavery, and Long for the Happy Day when I get to Sing along with the Trumpites, singing: ♫ *"I'm so Proud to be an American, where at least I Know that I am Free to Pay all of my Endless Bills, and to Consume all of my Countless Pills!"* Yes, that is like going to Heaven, until you reed: "Do People Go to Heaven when they Die?" (The Unbelievable Truth about Life and Death!) By The Good Pastor of Uncommon Sense! Book 120, and then you get Inspired to Build: "The Environmentalists' Perfect Paradise!" (HOW almost Everyone can be Living in a Beautiful Manmade Paradise!) By The Worldwide People's Revolution!® Book 035C, which is a Companion Book of: "The CONDENSED Version of MARK TWAIN Races for the PRESIDENCY with a Landslide VICTORY!" (The 2020 Presidential Candidates Desperately Need Some STRONG Undefeatable COMPETITION!) By The Worldwide People's Revolution!® Book 033C. After all, "Is America a White Nation with a Black Heart?" (How to Separate Truth from Fiction!) By The Good Pastor of Uncommon Sense! Book 118? Absolutely NOT! †§‡§§

P-[_] Most People have been Lying to themselves for Centuries: beCause of their PRIDE; but, now it is High Time for "The Great ATOMIC NIGHTMARE!" (The Saddest Story in

World History!) By The Great White Bald Eagle! Book 099, unless we Listen to: **"Our Selected King SPEAKS OUT!" (It is High Time for some Sane Person to get Total Control of this Insane World!) By The Worldwide People's Revolution!®** Book 100: beCause, there are no less than **"101 Good Reasons and Great Advantages for Establishing a Righteous One-World Government!" (Government By the People, Of the People, and For the People!) By The Worldwide People's Revolution!®** Book 104.

Q-[ ] I just LOVE those Delicious Swanky Dill Pickles with a Hot Pepper, Apple Cider Vinegar, and an Equal Amount of Montana Clover Honey, diluted with an equal amount of Spring Water, when the Pickles are Blended with Ripe (but, not overripe) Avocados, for a Wonderful Organic Corn Chip Dip, while Watching a Re-run of *The Ten Commandments* Movie by Cecil B. DeMille, who Produced the Best Movie ever made, called: *How the West was Won,* starring Jimmy Stewart, John Wayne, and other War Heroes. But, the Great Question is this: **"Are we just going to TALK about it, or take Action to bring it all about?"** Indeed, "Does a Good Soldier have to be a MURDERER?" (Seven Great Swanky Armies of

Voluntary Working Soldiers!) By The Worldwide People's Revolution!® Book 027B; or, can he not be a Good House Builder, like Jesus Christ, who Promoted "Beautiful Swanky Stone Dome Home COMPLEXES!" (HOW to Build SECURE Tax-proof, Insurance-proof, Self-air-conditioned, Paint-proof, Rot-proof, Termite-proof, Mouse-proof, Fireproof, Tornado-proof, Hurricane-proof, Thief-proof, and BOMB-PROOF Houses!) By The Worldwide People's Revolution!® Book 102, in *Matthew 7:24—25,* saying: *Therefore, whosoever Hears these Sayings of mine with his Spiritual Ears Wide Open, which are not Filled with the Wax of Unbelief, and also Does what I Teach, shall be Like a Wise Man, who Dug Down Deep into the Good Earth, and Built his House of Love on the Solid Bedrock of Divine Truths; and therefore, when the Lightning Struck, there was nothing to Light on Fire: beCause Rocks do not easily Burn; and when the Rains Descended, and the Floods came, there was nothing to be Washed Away: beCause a Mountainous Stone Fortress is no easy Thing to Conquer; and when the Fierce Winds Blew, and Beat upon that House, it did not Fall: beCause it was Founded on Provable Truths, which King Hadrian of Rome will Prove, when his Voluntary Army of Working Soldiers will Build the Pantheon, in Rome, which will be Standing there for a Testimony to what I Teach, which everyone in the Whole World could have, if they Elect to Establish a Righteous One-World Government: beCause there are Literally hundreds of thousands of Mountains of Rocks in this World of Wonders, which can be Used Wisely by Seven Great Armies of Working Soldiers, who can Invent and Produce the Correct Mechanical Slaves for Producing Beautiful Stone Dome Home Complexes with Home-craft Workshops, Well-made Tools, Sales Shops, and Spacious Kitchens, which Join Walk-in Root Cellars, Coolers and Freezers, which Join Luscious All-Mineral Organic Gardens, Vineyards and Orchards, which are Located on the Roofs of those Beautiful Stone Dome Home Complexes, which Drain into Large Cisterns for Water Storage, which Houses are Designed with THICK Stone Walls, so that they do not easily Heat Up nor Cool Down: beCause of being Self-air-conditioned, which are Built Up in Great Stone TERRACES, somewhat like these very Rough Drawings show:*

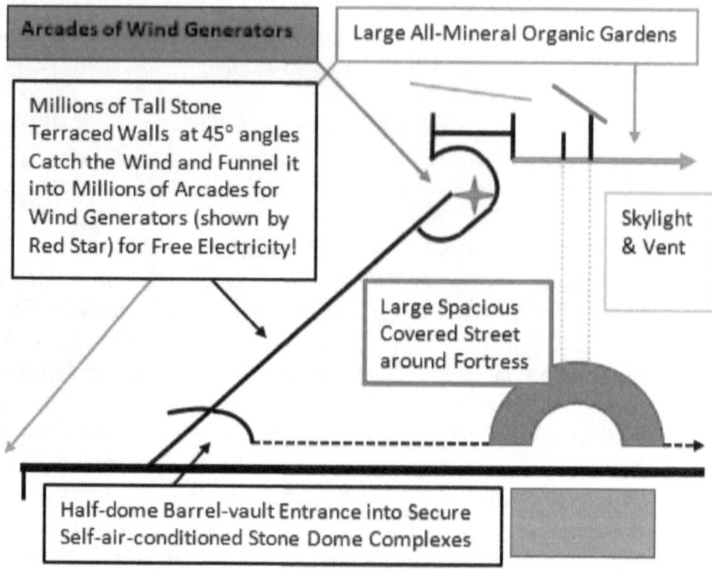

01-07 [_] Okay, O Evil Pastor of Common Sense, I have Heard all of the Lies that I care to Hear! Jesus did not Teach any such Provable Truths. Jesus did not give a Damn about Poor People, or else he would have told Saint Peter to get more Fishes with Money in their Mouths, whereby he might have given that Money to those Poor Beggars in Jerusalem, who had no Gardens to Eat from, nor any Government Food Stamps, Food Banks, nor Welfare Offices to Visit. Indeed, what Jesus needs to Do, is to Return to this Evil World, and Discover what a MESS it is now in — all beCause he Failed to Teach PROVABLE TRUTHS — such as People going to Heaven when they Die, rather than Pray, *"Thy Kingdom Come, O God, and your Will be Done on this Earth, even as it is now Done in Heavenly Places, like New Yuck City, Lungdung, Honk Konk, Lost Angels, Californicate, Mosque-cowardly, and Shitcago, Sicknoise."* — *The Mockingbird's Version.* †§‡§§

01-08 [_] Well, maybe you are not Crazy; but, you are Talking with a LOT of Crazy People, who cannot Understand what you are Saying: beCause they were not Tawt HOW to Reed Metaphors nor Understand Similes. Therefore, try not to Contaminate my Inspired Books with any Nasty Stuff that comes Out of the Anus of Chicago, Lost Angels, Californicate, nor New Yuck City — even though I dare say that 99.99% of those People can Understand that the Average American Wooden / Plastic Firetrap Mouse-infested Cockroach Den is not Worth used Toilet

Paper in a Severe Storm, Flood, Fire, Tornado, Hurricane, Mudslide, nor Earthquake: beCause they are Designed by Satan and Sons, Incorporated, who Rightfully Deserve to be Living in those Concrete Disasters when the Master Farmer Arises to SHAKE TERRIBLY the Whole Earth, whereby every Tall Wall and Tower will FALL, just as it is Written in: "The New MAGNIFIED Version of ISAIAH in Plain English!" (The Understandable Version of the Book of Isaiah!) By The Worldwide People's Revolution!® Book 044.

01-09 [_] O Good Pastor of Uncommon Sense, when that Dreadful Day comes, none of those "GLORIOUS Swanky Hotels Castles and Fortresses!" (Beautiful Planned City States for WISE Intelligent Well-Educated People with Common Sense and Good Understanding!) By The Worldwide People's Revolution!® Book 019B, will be Standing: beCause those Tall Stone Walls will FALL! †§‡

01-10 [_] Well, my Friend, the Good News about that Subject is this: Earthquakes have little or no Negative Effects on Underground Stone Dome Homes; but, if you Doubt it, ask the Park Rangers at Carlsbad Caverns, in New Mexico. For Example, that 100,000-gallon Cistern does not Leak. ‡

— Chapter 02 —

Does the Hopeless Church of Little Faith stand a Chance of Surviving the Great Famine?

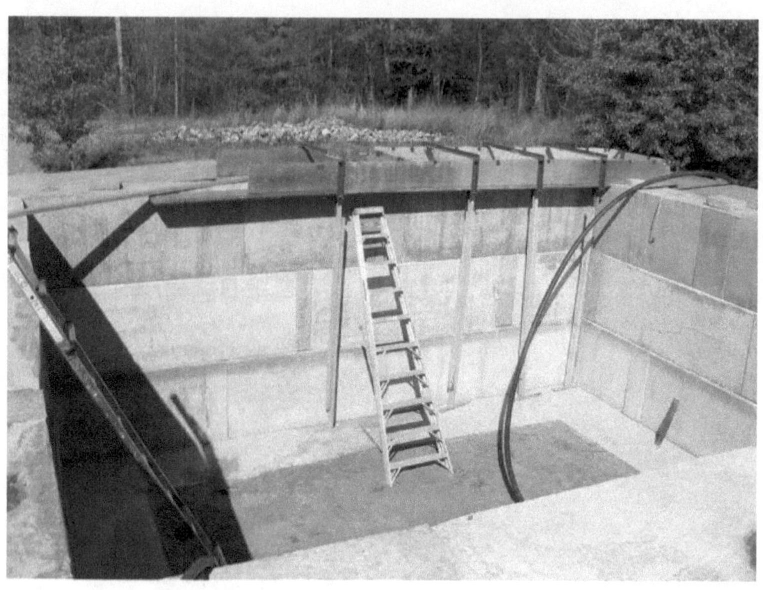

02-01 |_| Multitudes of Professing "Christians" have red the *Holy Bible,* and have even Heard about Climate Changes; but, they are Brutally Unaware that a Great Famine is Coming, when it will Stop Raining for 3.5 Years, according to *Revelation 11,* which you are welcome to pooh-pooh; but, **"What will you Do when the Rain STOPS?" (God's Last Resort to Save Mankind from his MADNESS!) By The Worldwide People's Revolution!®** Book 101? Awe, you will Rely on the False Government, right? Why not Rely on a Righteous Government, which would Immediately put a Billion or so Young Working Soldiers to WORK, Building those Swanky Cisterns for Water Storage, which can also be Used Wisely as "Batteries" for Storing Energy for Hydro-electric Power Plants? Why not Build those **"GLORIOUS Swanky Hotels Castles and Fortresses!" (Beautiful Planned City States for WISE Intelligent Well-Educated People with Common Sense and Good Understanding!) By The Worldwide People's Revolution!®** Book

019B, which will Solve no less than 5,000 Problems at the same Time, including all Unemployment Problems, forever? The Stonework will Represent the New Money, which will have to be Earned by Honest Labor, without any Loans, without any Interest / Usury, and without any Hateful Taxes: beCause, all of those Working Soldiers will Agree to Learn, Believe, Love, and OBEY **"The New MAGNIFIED Version of the 20 Commandments,"** which anyone can Discover in: **"LIGHTNING STRIKES Versus Lightning Bugs!" (HOW you can Become Moderately RICH, without Telling any Lies nor Selling any Trash!) By The Worldwide People's Revolution!®** Book 074, which anyone can Discover on Amazon dot com, if they Search for it; and, all Wise People will Search for it: beCause, it is one of the Best Books ever Written! ‡

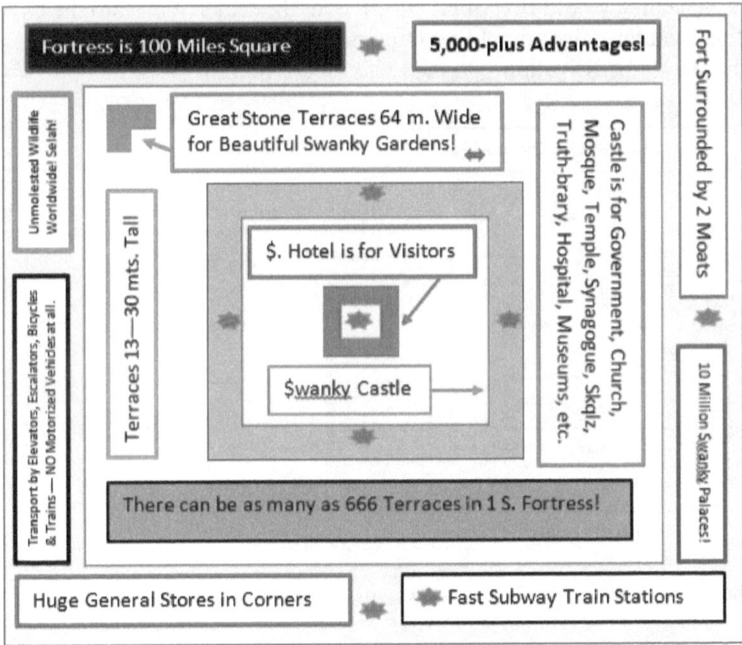

02-02 [_] O Good Pastor of Uncommon Sense, we have all Heard that same Song, before: beCause the Television Programs Advertise it every few Minutes: beCause that is one of the Great Benefits for the False Economic System, called: CAPITALISM, which is forever Seeking the Best Solutions for our Massive Problems, and then it Invests Billions of Dollars for Advertising those Best Solutions: beCause of having so much Love for ALL THAT IS GOOD! Yes, that is why we Hear so much about those: "Profitable Swanky MULCHING ROCKS!" (30 Advantages for Using Swanky Mulching Rocks in an All-Mineral Organic Garden!) By The Worldwide People's Revolution!® Book 098, which will make it Possible for us to have Weedless Gardens, which never Need HOEING! Moreover, you never have to Walk in the Mud, and your Fruits and Vegetables never get Dirty: beCause the Rainwater does not Splash Dirt onto the Fruits! Furthermore, your Children can Play in such a Garden, with Bare Feets, and never Worry about any Snakes Biting them: beCause of Living within those "GLORIOUS Swanky Hotels Castles and Fortresses!" (Beautiful Planned City States for WISE Intelligent Well-Educated People with Common Sense and Good Understanding!) By The Worldwide People's Revolution!® Book 019B, which are Surrounded by Deep MOATS, and Tall Stone Walls, 200 feet Tall, whereby not even Army Tanks can Cross over them: beCause they would first of all DROP over the Outer Wall into the Outer Moat, whereby they would be Drowned, and Eaten by the Algaegators, who would be Swimming in the Outermost Moat.

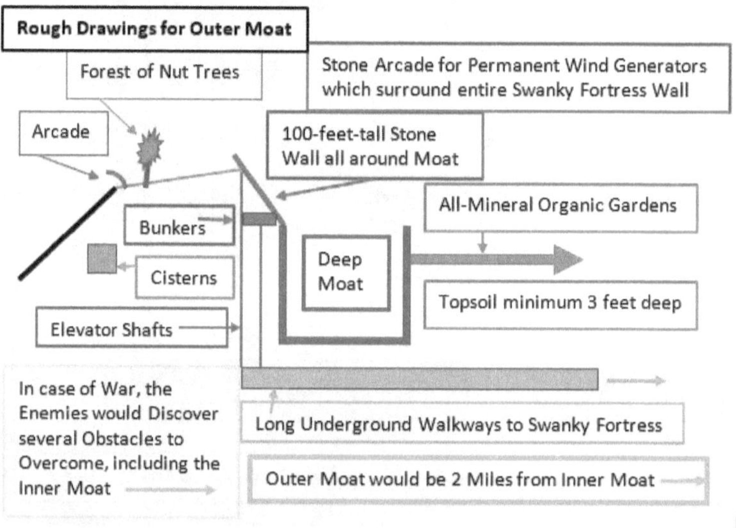

02-03 [_] So, O Good Pastor of Uncommon Sense, are you saying that "Seven Great Armies of Working Soldiers!" (HOW to Provide a Way for Everyone to WORK: so as to Eliminate Poverty, Crimes, Drug Abuses, Prisons and Unnecessary Taxes!) By The Worldwide People's Revolution!® Book 015B, should Immediately get to Work on the Construction of those Outer Moats for Swanky Fortresses, which are 100 Miles in Diameter!? Is that not going to Break the Banks?

02-04 [_] Well, my Friend, the First Thing that we, the People, will Do, is to Close the Doors on ALL Banks, Worldwide: beCause neither those Banks nor Bankers are Needed for True Prosperity: beCause, "**The New RIGHTEOUS One-World Government!**" (**HOW to Establish a Righteous One-World Government without Going to WAR!**) **By The Worldwide People's Revolution!**® Book 056, will simply OBEY: "**The CONSTITUTION for the New RIGHTEOUS One-World Government!**" (**HOW all Peoples can get True Justice, and Celebrate the Great Year of JUBILEE!**) **By The Worldwide People's Revolution!**® Book 016B, which will Solve the Money Problem, forever!

02-05 [_] O Good Pastor of Uncommon Sense, I want to See some Rough Drawings for the INNER Moat, just to See how STRONG and easy it will be to Defend, since the Outer Moat Looks very SECURE to me. In Fact, I have no Idea just HOW anyone could get Over it, Around it, nor Under it without being Detected by Sensors and Security Cameras, which would be Posted every 100 feet or so all around the Moat, which would be about 808 Miles Long, with no less than 42,666 Cameras and Bunkers for Guarding the Outside Perimeter of the Swanky Fortress — not to Mention the Inner Moat, which would have a Covered Highway with Ramparts!

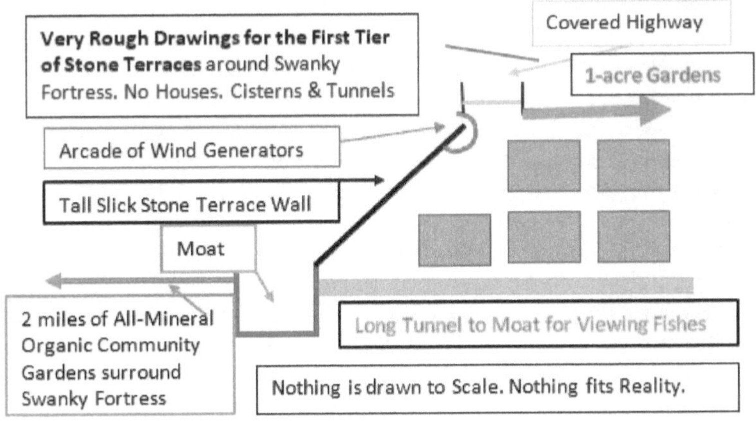

02-06 [_] Well, my Friend, there you have some very Rough Drawings of the Inner Moat and Tall SLICK Polished Granite Stone Wall, which no Murderous Army is going to Climb Over, if the Defenders are Prepared for them, Properly, which they would be at all Swanky

Fortresses, Worldwide: beCause that is the Best Way to Prevent any more Hateful Wars.

> IN JEFFERSON COUNTY, HOME TO THE LARGEST BLACK POPULATION IN KENTUCKY, THERE WILL BE ONE POLLING STATION FOR 616,000 REGISTERED VOTERS.

02-07 [_] O Good Pastor of Uncommon Sense, are you saying that Black People in the United States of America could Build their own Beautiful Planned City States; or, would they be Shipped back to Africa, where they Belong with other People of Like-mindedness, who are Busy Murdering one another, and Abusing themselves with Drugs: beCause they do not know how to Liv in Peace?

02-08 [_] Well, that would all Depend on what they Vote for: beCause they might be Happier to Liv in Africa, if we Help them to Build those **"GLORIOUS Swanky Hotels Castles and Fortresses!" (Beautiful Planned City States for WISE Intelligent Well-Educated People with Common Sense and Good Understanding!) By The Worldwide People's Revolution!® Book 019B**, all over Africa, if they Want them. After all, we are not going to FORCE People to Do what they do not Want to Do. In Fact, they are Welcome to continue to Liv in their Slums in Chicago, Illinois, Mississippi, Tennessee, Alabama, Georgia, or wherever they are now Living. However, I would Think that they would Gladly Join those **"Seven Great Armies of Working Soldiers!" (HOW to Provide a Way for Everyone to WORK: so as to Eliminate Poverty, Crimes, Drug Abuses, Prisons and Unnecessary Taxes!) By The Worldwide People's Revolution!® Book 015B**, and thus, put an End to **"Poverty Hunger Riots Strikes Police Brutalities Election Deceptions and Civil Wars!" (The High Price that we Earthlings have Paid for Leaving the Good Land!) By The Worldwide People's Revolution!® Book 014B**. After all, it is now Possible and most Practical for every Family to Liv in those **"Beautiful Swanky PALACES!" (A New Concept in Living Habits — Swanky Palaces for Poor People!) By The Worldwide People's Revolution!® Book 066**, just by Exercising their DUMBmocracy, and go to the Polls to: **"VOTE for The GOAT!" (The New Political Party that has**

Guaranteed Solutions for our Massive Problems!) By The Worldwide People's Revolution!® Book 109, which is WHY that they should Study: "MARK TWAIN Races for the PRESIDENCY with a Landslide VICTORY!" (The 2020 Presidential Candidates Desperately Need Some STRONG Undefeatable COMPETITION!) By The Worldwide People's Revolution!® Book 033B. †§‡

02-09 [_] O Good Pastor of Uncommon Sense, those Stupid Ignorant Niggers could never Manage to Build their own Swanky Palaces without the Help of White Architects and Engineers. †§‡§§

02-10 [_] Well, my Potential Enemy, you should not Speak Evil of those Black People: beCause they were Born to be Good Servants, for the most Part, and a few of them were Born to be Good Masters, even as it is among ALL of the Races; but, a White Nigger like Donald Trump is not Qualified to be a Master of any Kind, unless he Repents of all of his Sins, and Straightens himself out. After all, he still has some 3,000-plus Lawsuits Filed against him for Robbing his Employees, if the Reports are True; and they most likely are True. Indeed, President Trump is a New York City Con Artist, according to many Reports, which should be Investigated by someone other than the Federal Burden of False Investigators, who did not even Discover the Chief Terrorists, who Sliced Off that Hardened Steel Column at the World Trade Center during September 11, 2001.†§‡

Take a Better Look, O you Extremely Ignorant Fools!

{Do you Think that such a Hardened Steel Column Sliced Off itself at a 45-degree Angle? Why do you not DEMAND: "The GREAT Worldwide TELEVISED Court HEARING!" (That Great Meeting of the Most-Intelligent and Well-Educated Minds!) By The Worldwide People's Revolution!® Book 041B, whereby you might Learn the Whole Truth about it, and your FAKE Government? Why do you not Ask your Friends, Relatives, and Naaberz to Please Explain just HOW that Hardened Steel Column got itself Sliced Off? Trust me, it was not done by any Airplanes; but, it was done by Military-grade Nano-Thermite (in a Controlled Demolition Project), which only the Military had Access to. Therefore, the Federal Government of "The Divided States of United Lies!" (The so-called "United States of North America" in Disguise!) By The Worldwide People's Revolution!® Book 058, was Totally Responsible for it, which can be Proven in a Courtroom, if anyone is Interested in Justice for ALL, including those Poor Black People, who Desperately Need some GOOD Masters, who should Study: "A Sound Argument for Good Masters and Obedient Servants!" (WHY Everyone Needs a Good Master, and every Master Needs Good Obedient Servants!) By The Worldwide People's Revolution!® Book 008B, and: "Is America a White Nation with a Black Heart?" (How to Separate Truth from Fiction!) By The Good Pastor of Uncommon Sense! Book 118, which will not Burn Out your Eyeballs to Read it. Therefore, Educate yourselves, O you Low-Class IGNORANT FOOLS! See YouTube for: **"Experts Speak Out!"**}

— Chapter 03 —

Will the Hopeless Church of Little Faith Build any Swanky Fortresses?

03-01 [_] Jesus said, *"They have Ears; but, behold, they cannot Hear very Well; and they have Eyes, but they cannot See very Well: beCause they are Spiritually Blinded by their Pride."* — *The Gospel of Saint Thomas.* Therefore, will they have any Faith in "The Right Design for Living!" (A List of 5,000 Advantages for Building Beautiful Planned City States!) By The Worldwide People's Revolution!® Book 012C? NO, they will NOT: beCause, *"They are Looking for a Holy City that is made without Hands, whose Builder and Maker is GOD,"* they say. However, they are not Qualified to Liv in any such Holy Cities, by Reason of the Fact that they are Liars and Hypocrites, who Say that they Love God, while Disobeying his Commandments — one of which is to, *"Come you Out from among the Wicked Ones, and be you Separated from them, says the Supreme Ruler and Divine Lawmaker; and Touch NONE of their Unclean Things, and then I will Receive you, and will be a Loving Father unto you, and you shall become my Chosen Sons and Purified Dawterz, says the Almighty God. Otherwise, you shall be Cast into an Horrible Place, which is like a Lake of Fire that is Burning with Stinking Sulfur, where you shall make yourselves into Slaves of an Evil Empire, while Singing: ♫ 'I'm so Proud to be an American, where at least I Know that I am Free to Pay all of my Endless Bills, and Consume all of my Countless Pills: beCause I am not at all Deceived by any Means: beCause I Pledge my Allegiance to a Bloody Rag with 50 White Stars and 13 Stripes,'* which goes on to Repeat itself." — *The Mockingbird's Version*

03-02 [_] O Good Pastor of Uncommon Sense, the Trumpites and Edomites will not Like that Verse, and are likely to Hire some Assassinator to Murder you for it: beCause they are Patriotic Americans, who have their Heads Stuck in one or the other of those 2 Stinking Holes, in: "The BIG White OUTHOUSE on the Not-so-Biblical Capitol DUNGHILL!" (The Chief Sins of the Divided States of United Lies!) By The Worldwide People's Revolution!® Book 023B. §‡

03-03 [_] Well, my Friend, it is quite Difficult to Kill a Dead Man, who is Speaking from his Grave, whose Voice will be Heard all around the World: beCause his Spiritual Children will Learn the Truth that he has

Learned, and will thus March in Great Parades in Honor of him and his Inspired Books of Provable Truths, while they Pass Out Free Literature on the Streets, to whomever has Spiritual Ears that can Hear. {See: "Hosts of **HOAXES Live In Under Around and Over the Little White OUTHOUSE!**" (WHY Spiritually-Blind Cowardly-Americans are Hunkering Down in their Empty Root Cellars!) **By The Irreverent Penname Oversight!** Book 111.}

03-04 [_] If you do not Think that Swanky Fortresses are Necessary, you should Watch this Video: https://youtu.be/-fusUxEPwsw Rubber Tires — a very Dirty Business | DW Documentary.

03-05 [_] O Good Pastor of Uncommon Sense, you should Study: "The Nature of CAPITALISM!" (A List of the EVILS of CAPITALISM!) By The Worldwide People's Revolution!® B-038, which could be Magnified into an Encyclopedia of EVILS: beCause there are so many of those Evils to List, which would Require several thousand Researchers a Decade or more to Discover all of the Evils, and get them Documented in Video Programs for YouTube. In Fact, the Capitalists would likely be Inventing more Evils, Daily, than could be Documented in one Year: beCause that is the Nature of GREED. For Example, see https://youtu.be/AFfi6H4Heyw The Sugar Capital of Australia. As it is, Australia is Surrounded by Oceans of Water, some of which could be Distilled by Solar Power in the Vast Deserts of Australia; but, the Poor Government cannot Afford to do that for the Poor Farmers: beCause the Fake Government has Bought into the Edomite Capitalist Economic System, which Services the Rich Bankers, as Usual, as Normal. †§‡

03-06 [_] Well, my Friend, for the most part, Capitalism is a Century Late and a Trillion Dollars Short. The Amount of Juice in the Sugarcane Naturally Depends on the Amount of Water in the Ground. In other Words, more Water in the Fields, means more Juice in the Sugarcanes. But, the Problem is the Fact that all such Highly-Refined Sugar is an Abomination for Ignorant People to Eat: beCause it Rots the Teeth, Reverses the Pancreas, and Causes Diabetes, according to certain Scientists, who Study the EVILS of the Sugar Industry. However, the Consumers do not pay much Attention to those Scientists, Dentists, nor Honest Authors: beCause the Sugar Industry is Sanctioned, Approved, Authorized, and Promoted by the Anti-Christ False Government, which does whatever is Necessary for Producing Extreme Poverty, Higher Taxes, Low-grade Products, and Endless Pollution. For Example, see: https://youtu.be/c94QFkV-s18 Harvesting Giants — High-Tech for Farmers | Full Exceptional Engineering Documentary on YouTube. The

Mechanical Accomplishments of Mankind are Most Marvelous, when you Think about them; but, what about the Necessary Connection between Mankind and the Land, Plants, Animals, and each other? It is no Secret that Gardeners are Closer to God: beCause of being Closer to Nature's God. Indeed, there is a Direct Connection between Sanity and Nature, which is most Important for Children, who Need to be Bonded to the Natural World, without which they are more likely to become Rebellious Criminals of Various Kinds. Just a Pet, a few Trees, a Garden, a few Chickens, Ducks, or a Bird in a Cage is Better than nothing for Bonding People with God, which is WHY People made Public Parks, Flower Gardens, Zoos, Ponds and Swimming Pools: beCause of Realizing the Need for Natural Surroundings, in order to Maintain Sanity, which is WHY that God makes Sure that X-number of Rebellious Spirits are Born on Farms and Ranches, whereby they might be Corrected by Nature, and Tawt all Kinds of Good Lessons, while Satan is Busy making Enemies and Wars, and then Reporting Propagandist Lies about it all, for Covering Up their Evil Deeds, which are often Exposed by Honest Authors — such as Charles Hanley, who wrote about the Korean War in his book, called: *Ghost Flames,* which Exposes American Governmental Sins. †§‡

03-07 [_] O Good Pastor of Uncommon Sense, do you Think that the People of this World of Woes will ever come to their Riit Senses, and Build those **"GLORIOUS Swanky Hotels Castles and Fortresses!"** **(Beautiful Planned City States for WISE Intelligent Well-Educated People with Common Sense and Good Understanding!) By The Worldwide People's Revolution!®** Book 019B? Do you Think that they will ever Realize the Impossibility of Conquering a Swanky Fortress from the Outside? For Example, 250 or more Russian Soldiers Lost their Lives in an Attempt to Conquer Himmler's House in Berlin, Germany, at the End of World War 2, while the Germans Lost NONE: beCause, they finally ran out of Ammunition, and thus, Surrendered to the Russians, which would be the same Case in an Attempt to Conquer those "Beautiful Swanky Stone Dome Home COMPLEXES!" (HOW to Build SECURE Tax-proof, Insurance-proof, Self-air-conditioned, Paint-proof, Rot-proof, Termite-proof, Mouse-proof, Fireproof, Tornado-proof, Hurricane-proof, Thief-proof, and BOMB-PROOF Houses!) By The Worldwide People's Revolution!® Book 102, which would be 10 Times more Difficult to Conquer than Himmler's House: beCause of being Designed for Good Self-Defense.

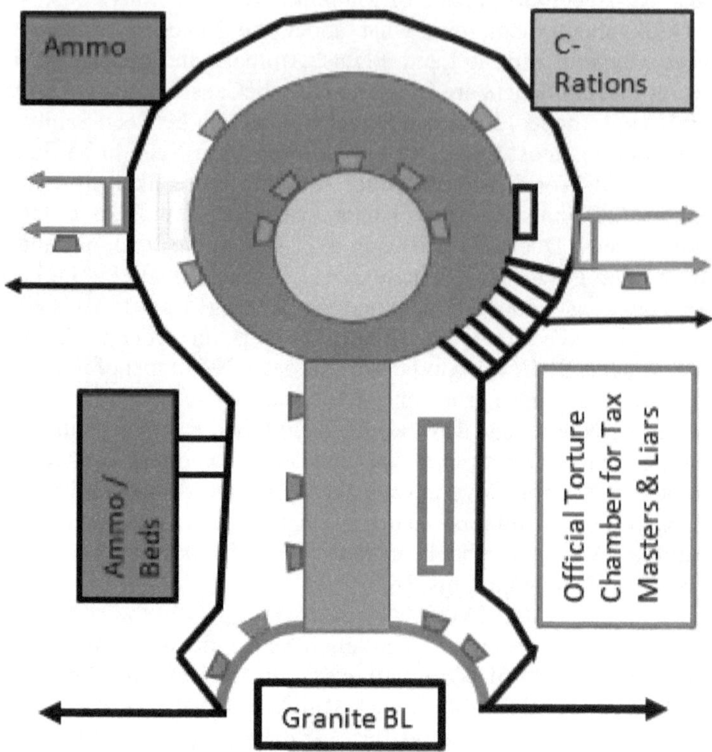

03-08 [_] Well, my Friend, even if the Enemy got into the Swanky Fortress by Parachutes, they would be up against Insurmountable Odds, just to get Into one of those Well-Defended Entrances into a Swanky Stone Dome Home Complex: beCause the Balcony would provide the "High Ground," while the Entrance would prove to be a TRAP: beCause, once the Enemy gets into the Entrance Dome, the large Granite Block would prevent them from Escaping, when it Quietly Rolls against the Barrel-vault Tunnel, and sets itself down there. Therefore, the Enemies would have to Surrender, or else be Destroyed in the Trap: beCause there would be no Place for them to Hide. ‡

03-09 [_] O Good Pastor of Uncommon Sense, the Enemy could drop big Bombs on all of the Gardens, Vineyards, and Orchards within a Swanky Fortress, whereby they could be Starved Out.

03-10 [_] Well, my Friend, the Swanky Fortresses would have Good Food Supplies for every Family, and for at least 10 Years. However,

Bombing the Gardens would Prove to be a Grave Mistake, when those Gardens would be the Primary Food Supplies for the Outside World: beCause no one would Want to Eat the Garbage Foods that are found in Gross Grocery Stores, once they got a Good Taste of Swanky Foods. Therefore, given a few Years, most People would be Relying on Swanky Fortress Gardens. Therefore, nothing would be Gained by Bombing them. †§‡

— Chapter 04 —

Why would anyone Attack a Swanky Fortress?

04-01 [_] It is Expected that many Edomites will be Unhappy with the Fact that their Evil Empire has been Destroyed by "The Swanky Sword of Divine Truths!" (The Most-Powerful Weapon in the Whole Universe!) By The Worldwide People's Revolution!® Book 067, in a Courtroom: beCause of finding them Guilty of War Crimes, Banker Crimes, Industrial Crimes, Slave Labor Crimes, Healthcare Crimes, Fake Education Crimes, and so on — even a whole Long List of CRIMES against Humanity, which were never Needed for Prosperity: beCause it was always Possible, ever since the Industrial Revolution, for everyone to be Moderately RICH; but, the Lying Conniving Edomites were Greedy, Selfish People, who Wanted all of the Wealth for themselves: beCause they have no Love nor Compassion for the Masses of People, whom they Seek to make into their SLAVES of Various Kinds, beginning with Education Slaves, when no such Slavery is Required for True Prosperity: beCause, it does not Require a College Diploma to Mix Up some Concrete and Build a House; but, it Requires about 99% Work, and 1% Brain Power, even as it also Requires to Read a Gardening Book, and Do some All-Mineral Organic Gardening, with the Assistance of **"The Swanky Association of Professional All-Mineral Organic Gardeners,"** who are Happy to Teach Children HOW: beCause, it is Good that Children Learn how to Feed themselves, which is much more Important than Learning how to Color Drawings in School Books, which do not Profit anyone anything, even as Swinging in a Swing does not Profit anyone anything, when that Time and Energy can be Spent Wisely, Picking Blueberries and Raspberries, for example, whereby a Child can Feel Good about himself, as a Productive Member of Society, and not just another Leech on Society. However, that is not to say that Children should not be Tawt how to Reed and Riit: beCause that is also Necessary; but, it is not Necessary to Waste 10 to 20 Years in "The Public School of IGNERUNT FQLZ!" (HOW we have been GRAATLEE DISEEVD by Capitalism!) By The Worldwide People's Revolution!® Book 024B, whereby a Person can be made into an Education Slave, Work Slave, Tax Slave, Insurance Slave, Rent Slave, Credit Card Debt Slave, Home-owner Slave, Interest Slave, Mortgage Slave, Transportation Slave, Repair Bills Slave, ElecTrickery Bills Slave, Food Bills Slave, Water Bills Slave, Gas Bills Slave,

Entertainment Bills Slave, Drug Bills Slave, Doctor Bills Slave, Hospital Bills Slave, Childcare Bills Slave, Nursery Home Bills Slave, and Funeral Home Bills Slave: beCause none of that is Necessary for Living within "Beautiful Swanky PALACES!" (A New Concept in Living Habits — Swanky Palaces for Poor People!) By The Worldwide People's Revolution!® Book 066. Indeed, with only 6 Years of Common Skilled Labor, a Person should be Set Up for Living like a Rich Person, whereby he can Attend to his own Garden of Eden, and Liv and Work at Home with his own Family and Friends, without Buying any Ugly Firetrap Mouse-infested Cockroach Den to Liv in, which has Unnecessary Heating and Cooling Bills: beCause of making THICK Stone Walls, which Stabilize the Temperatures, and Provide Consistent Temperatures the Year Around, by Building Ice Houses, which Suck Out the Moisture during Hot Summers, while also Cooling the House, if it is Needed: beCause of having an Unlimited Supply of FREE Electricity. {See the Drawings just before Verse 01-07, and Understand that we can make Billions of Stone Wind Funnels at the Tops of Tall Stone Walls, in Arcades, just to have that Free ElecTrickery, without making Slaves of anyone: beCause Mechanical Slaves can do 95% of the Difficult Work for us, which is what Tools are Good for. Therefore, instead of Producing 250-million-dollar Jet Bombers, we can Produce 250 Swanky Rock-cutting Machines, or 250,000 Swanky Rock-polishing Machines, or 2 Million Swanky Electric Roto-Tillers for Mixing Compost with Topsoil.

04-02 [_] So, O Good Pastor of Uncommon Sense, are you saying that we could get everyone in the Whole World SET UP for Proper Living, at HOME, whereby no one would have to go Looking for a Boring Job, just to Liv within those "Beautiful Swanky PALACES!" (A New Concept in Living Habits — Swanky Palaces for Poor People!) By The Worldwide People's Revolution!® Book 066? WHO would Manage such Construction Projects, seeing that no such Palaces have ever been Built?

04-03 [_] Well, my Friend, the Extra-Bright Students in Schools will Cheerfully Volunteer to Learn HOW to Manage such Construction Projects. Therefore, Teachers and Professors will have to be Tawt HOW, first, who can then Teach their Students HOW, who can all Join: **"Seven Great Armies of Working Soldiers!"** (HOW to Provide a Way for **Everyone to WORK: so as to Eliminate Poverty, Crimes, Drug Abuses, Prisons and Unnecessary Taxes!) By The Worldwide People's Revolution!®** Book 015B, until the Palaces get Built; and then they can Join: **"The Swanky Associations of Working Soldiers!" (A Fascinating Collection of Various Kinds of Voluntary Working Soldiers!) By The Worldwide People's Revolution!®** Book 018B, whereby they can Contribute their 4 Hours of Common Skilled Labor per Workday, and have the Remainder of their Time Off, which they can Use Wisely for Studying Good Books, going to Schools, Playing Music, or just Watching Movies, if that is what they Choose to Do: beCause, if they do their 4 Hours of Common Skilled Labor, Correctly, everyone will Prosper. For Example, how Long do you Think it would Require for you to put that Potato-Avocado Salad Together, if 4 other People Furnished you with the Ingredients? Probably one Hour, at the most, if you took your sweet Time about it. Therefore, if you made 4 Times that much Salad in 4 Hours, you could Feed 16 People a Wholesome Lunch, and you would hardly make a Dent in those Baskets of Potatoes, which you can see just after Verse 01-06G, which our Selected King Dug Up with a Potato Digging Fork in less than 4 Hours, and Washed all of them during the next 4 Hours, while sitting under his Fig Tree, in the Shade. Therefore, if each Working Soldier Contributes his Daily Share of the

Labor to the Cause, everyone can Eat at those "Royal Swanky Buffets!" (The Best Feasts in the Whole World!) By The Worldwide People's Revolution!® Book 103, for FREE! Moreover, **"The Swanky Association of House Cleaners"** will keep all of the Houses Clean, and without Using any Stinking Toxic Perfumes, Lie-sol, nor any other Abominations: beCause, in most Cases, just plain Pure Water will Work Well for Cleaning Houses and Windows; but, if not, just a little Vinegar will Help; or, some Natural Dr. Bronner's Soap, which can also be Used for Washing the Clothes; but, not any of those Stinking Perfumed Soaps, which are Inventions of Satan and Dawterz, Incorporated. †§‡

04-04 [_] So, O Good Pastor of Uncommon Sense, what about Disinfectants for Viirusez, Germs, Bacterias, and other Enemies of Mankind — such as Athlete's Foot Disease?

04-05 [_] Well, my Friend, you can Kill such Germs with Hydrogen Peroxide, Alcohol, Vinegar, or Dr. Bronner's Soap; but, if not, it is Time for the Victim of Capitalism to FAST and PRAY: beCause that is a Guaranteed Solution for whatever Ails Mankind, if it is Done Correctly, which is God's Solution. Therefore, you should Study: "The Proper RULES for FASTING!" (The Complete Instruction Manual for True Repentance!) By The Worldwide People's Revolution!® Book 046, which is a Companion Book of: "HOW to Become a HOLY Man!" (40 Good Reasons WHY People Should FAST and PRAY!) By The Worldwide People's Revolution!® Book 045. Just Remember that our Selected King has not Consumed any Medicines in more than 50 Years, and has not had the Flu in more than 50 Years! †§‡

04-06 [_] O Good Pastor of Uncommon Sense, if a Wild Animal gets Sick or Badly Wounded, it will just Stop Eating: beCause of Losing its Appetite, whereby it will soon get Well again, which is Nature's One and ONLY Remedy. Therefore, it only seems to be Reasonable that the same Remedy will Work for People, if they just Follow the RULES! Indeed, it is one of those Things that we can easily Prove at: "The GREAT Worldwide TELEVISED Court HEARING!" (That Great Meeting of the Most-Intelligent and Well-Educated Minds!) By The Worldwide People's Revolution!® Book 041B. In Fact, I Volunteer to be the First "Guinea Pig" to Prove it.‡

04-07 [_] Well, my Friend, that would be a Good Reason for the Edomites to Cook Up another Hateful War, and Attack a Swanky Fortress, if we can Prove that Medical Snakes are not Needed for Obtaining and Maintaining Good Health, who have found Faults with:

"Did God or Satan Ordain Medical Doctors?" (Ask Huck Finn and/or Nigger Jim: because neither Tom Sawyer nor Judge Thatcher would Know!) By The Worldwide People's Revolution!® Book 022B. ‡

04-08 [_] O Good Pastor of Uncommon Sense, are you saying that we will not even Need Medical Doctors for Mending the People, who have gotten into Bad Car Accidents within Swanky Fortresses, at Race Tracks? And what about those Athletes, who are Injured while Playing Ball Games, Gymnastics, Ice Hockey, Football, Boxing, Tennis, Basketball, and other Violent Sports? What about Syphilis, Gonorrhea, and other Dangerous Sexual Diseases — will there be no Medical Doctors to Heal them? †§‡§§

04-09 [_] Well, my Friend, if anyone Wants to Gamble with their Health, and Play Dangerous Sports, they will have to Leave Swanky Fortresses to Do it: beCause we will Try to Avoid all Dangers, and have no Race Tracks, Violent Sports, nor any Competition at all: beCause that is only another Deception of Satan, to Build Up People's Pride, and make Fools of them, while Depressing the "Losers," who can all be Winners, just by Studying our Selected King's Inspired Books, and then Obeying them. ‡

04-10 [_] O Good Pastor of Uncommon Sense, with such a System as you Propose, no one will be Willing to Defend any Swanky Fortresses: beCause they will not have enough Pride in themselves to Defend themselves. †§‡

— Chapter 05 —

Will Swanky Fortresses not be Competing with other Swanky Fortresses?

05-01 [_] O Good Pastor of Uncommon Sense, let us see what Mr. Google has to say about Competition, if you do not Object to Learning a few Important Things.

Healthy **competition** inspires kids to do their best – not just **good** enough. When students **compete** they will become more inquisitive, research independently, and learn to work with others. They will strive to do more than is required.

www.ineos.com › inch-magazine › articles › issue-5 › d... ▾
Debate: Is Competition good for kids? - Ineos
Is competition a good thing?

You know you have a **good** idea when other people are coming up with similar products or services. **Competition** validates the market and the fact that there are most likely customers for your new product. This also means that the costs of marketing and educating your market goes down (see my next point).

articles.bplans.com › why-competition-is-a-good-thing
Why Competition is a Good Thing - Bplans Blog

05-02 [_] For Example, when our Selected King built his 100,000-gallon Cistern for Water Storage, he Knew that he had a Bad Idea: beCause no one else was Competing with him. †§‡§§

What are the positive effects of competition?

These benefits include increased productivity resulting from cooperative teamwork and mutual efforts. Additionally, a team can expect to produce higher quality output because **positive competition** often results in increased motivation, innovation, and creativity necessary to improve processes and results. Dec 21, 2009

www.brighthubpm.com › resource-management › 59735-...
Positive and Negative Competition: Influences on Project Team ...

05-03 [_] For Example, beCause no one was Competing with our Selected King, to build any large Cisterns for Water Storage, no other such Cisterns got Built in "The Divided States of United Lies!" (The so-called "United States of North America" in Disguise!) By The

Worldwide People's Revolution!® Book 058, in spite of the Fact that Billions of such Cisterns are Needed, just in case the Rain might Stop, and the Masses of Ignorant People might Starve to Death! †§‡§§

Why is competition not good?

Competition is destructive to children's self-esteem, it interferes with learning, sabotages relationships, and **isn't** necessary to have a **good** time.

www.alfiekohn.org › article › case-competition
The Case Against Competition - Alfie Kohn

05-04 [_] I did not take the Time to read that Website; but, I am Sure that there is a Mountain of Evidences to Prove that Competition can Destroy Innocent Children. In Fact, there is a Good Chance that President Donald Jaywalking Trump is a Victim of Competition, which has Caused him to be such a Narcissistic Person, who has Referred to "those A-hole countries over there." †§‡

Is competition good for success?

Competition teaches us about goal setting. Creating and setting goals is an important part of being in any competitive landscape. ... Goals created for **competition** contribute to building persistence and determination as individuals increase their challenges and develop a mindset focused for **success**. Nov 25, 2016

leaderonomics.com › necessity-competition-leadership
Why Competition is Necessary for the Leaders of Tomorrow ...

05-05 [_] *"Do with all of your Might whatsoever your Hands Discover to Do, as if Doing it for God, and not for Vain Men, who have no Idea what they might Accomplish, if they had such a Good Attitude,"* which might make them far more Successful. ‡

Competition is part of our DNA. **Competition** is a **necessary** part of our everyday lives. After all, evolutionary theory tells us that even from the earliest days of our existence, every species is consistently engaged in a **competitive** struggle for **life** on earth. Healthy **competition** is good for all. Nov 25, 2016

leaderonomics.com › necessity-competition-leadership
Why Competition is Necessary for the Leaders of Tomorrow ...

05-06 [_] Competition and Stress has no doubt Shortened the Lives of everyone who got Deceived by it, including the Lions and Bears. People who never have to Compete, have Historically Lived much Longer,

Healthier Lives than those under Severe Stress and Competition to Win.
†§‡

The Pros and Cons of Being Competitive

- Pro: It motivates you to work harder. Setting your goals higher than your classmate or friend's can help you work harder and as a result, do better. ...
- Con: The pressure can get to you. ...
- Pro: It's exciting. ...
- Con: It can put a dent on relationships. ...
- Pro: You become more focused. ...
- Con: You get consumed with bitterness.

05-07 |_| Very few People in all of History have done as much Hard Work as our Selected King, who was not Competing with anyone in **"The Process of Making a RIGHTEOUS KING!" (A Fascinating Autobiography of our Selected King!) By The Worldwide People's Revolution!® Book 082. See: "LIGHTNING STRIKES Versus Lightning Bugs!" (HOW you can Become Moderately RICH, without Telling any Lies nor Selling any Trash!) By The Worldwide People's Revolution!®** Book 074, for the Proof. The Pressure of Competing can Kill you with a Heart Attack. The Excitement of Winning can Build Up your Pride, which can also Kill you. Competition can Ruin Friendships. You can become so Focused, that you become like Donald Trump, who puts his own Interests above those of the Masses of People. Becoming a Loser in the Game of Competition can Cause you to Commit Suicide! †§‡

Competition, Attention, and Memory. Our results support the notion that a **competitive** environment can **affect** memory and effort. ... More likely, however, **competition** may only **affect** performance on a physical effort task in an environment where **competitors** **compete** side-by-side, which **did** not occur in our task. Sep 1, 2015

www.ncbi.nlm.nih.gov › pmc › articles › PMC4554955
The power of competition: Effects of social motivation on attention

the **purpose of competition** is for businesses to try to outdo each other in order to earn more. By doing this, businesses will come up with newer ways to please their customers.

brainly.com › question
What is the purpose of competition? a. to act as a regulating force

05-08 |_| It is more likely that Competition will Cause Businessmen to Cheat in Various Ways, in order to Earn more Money, which is the

Common Evil Thing among all such Competitors. For Example, Tires have Expiration Dates, which are often Coded and printed in Tiny Letters on their Tires: beCause they do not Want their Customers to Learn how Old those Tires are. Nevertheless, it should be the Law that their Expiration Dates should be as Big as their Brand Names, whereby their Customers might Realize how Badly they are getting Robbed, and Decide to Move into Swanky Fortresses, where there is no Need for Cars nor Trucks of any Kind. Moreover, there are no Traffic Accidents, no Traffic Jams, no Traffic Tickets, and the Trains are always on Time. †§‡

Competitions offer **a** chance for participants **to** gain substantial experience, showcase skills, analyze and evaluate outcomes and uncover personal aptitude. **Competitions** also encourage students **to** adopt innovative techniques and develop their ideas and skills. Jun 24, 2019

studentcompetitions.com › posts › how-participating-in-c...
How Participating In Competitions Can Benefit Your Student Life ...

05-09 [ ] Working Soldiers at Swanky Fortresses are not Motivated by Gaining Money, which gives to them an entire Book full of Advantages over the Proud Person, who is Motivated by Money, and has no Real Interest in Helping the People. See: "For the Love of Money!" (The Strange Things that People Say and Do to Get more Money!) By The Worldwide People's Revolution!® Book 003B, which is a Companion Book of: "The Root Cause for almost all Evils!" (The Strange Things that People Say and Do to Get more Money!) By The Worldwide People's Revolution!® Book 078. The Love of Money was the Reason for Capitalists to Dump their Toxic Chemical Poisons and Trash into the Rivers, Lakes, Seas and Oceans. The United States has more than 10,000 Landfills for Capitalist Trash, which was never Needed for True Prosperity. Swanky Fortresses would have ZERO Trash Dumps, as it should be Worldwide. Musical Instruments can be Recycled, if they get Worn Out. Glass Canning Jars can also be Recycled. Kitchen Garbage will be Composted with Treated Dung and Diluted Piss. †§‡

The **U.S.** has 3,091 active **landfills** and over 10,000 old municipal **landfills**, according to the Environmental Protection Agency.

www.zerowasteamerica.org › Landfills
LANDFILLS - Zero Waste America

The **United States** contributes as **much** as 242 million pounds of plastic **trash** to the **ocean** every year, according to that study. China has begun to take steps to stem the tide of **trash** floating from its shores. Sep 7, 2018

www.usatoday.com › story › tech › science › 2018/09/07
Great Pacific Garbage Patch: Where did all the trash come from?

05-10 [_] Capitalism has no Plans for Abandoning the Production of more Capitalist Trash. See: https://youtu.be/Vu1sPAqP0uM Child Labor for Shimmering Cosmetics.

Being competitive also has its disadvantages such as people **being** labeled as conceited, self absorbed, too picky, full of themselves and not **being** flexible and sometimes passive aggressive. Feb 25, 2016

www.huffpost.com › entry › the-pros-and-cons-of-havi_b...
The Pros and Cons of Having a Competitive Personality | HuffPost

05-11 [_] President Trump is a Perfect Example of a Competitive Capitalist, who Believes that Gain is Godliness. †§‡

First, **negative competition** fosters hostility, anger, and pessimism, which leads to increased instances of stress and physical ailments. Unhealthy **competition** also negatively influences a team's morale and team-based spirit, therefore negatively affecting productivity, teamwork, and cooperation. Dec 21, 2009

www.brighthubpm.com › resource-management › 59735-...
Positive and Negative Competition: Influences on Project Team ...

05-12 [_] It would be Difficult to Judge just Exactly how BAD Competition is; but, if you Watch the above Link in Verse 05-10, you will Understand some of the Evils of Capitalism. (Check the above Box, only if you have Watched that Video.)

Disadvantages of competition in education process

- STRESS OFTEN COMES HAND-IN-HAND WITH COMPETITION ✓✓ Competition can easily lead to stress and anxiety, especially if it promotes academic competition between individual students. ...
- BE PREPARED FOR DISAPPOINTMENT ✓✓ ...
- UNHEALTHY COMPETITION LEADS TO LOWER ENGAGEMENT ✓✓

However, the psychological trait of **competitiveness** often has nothing to do with survival, although the tendency to **compete** might be a natural outgrowth of biological **competition**. Healthy levels of **competition** can help improve self-esteem and increase enjoyment of life. Jul 18, 2019

www.goodtherapy.org › blog › psychpedia › competitive...
Competitiveness - GoodTherapy

Not **everything** in life is **competition**.

Because they come easy. You only find completion in the beautiful stuff which you want in your life and thus the others too. And that's the best part about those things which make them precious to us because we have fought for it and achieved it.

www.quora.com › Why-is-everything-in-life-a-competition
Why is everything in life a competition? - Quora

When overseen by appropriate adults, **competition** can build self-esteem, teach valuable life skills and positively shape a child's life. In it's healthier version, **competition** is absolutely necessary for an athlete to reach higher and achieve his/her goals. Feb 3, 2016

www.competitivedge.com › is-competition-good-or-bad
IS COMPETITION GOOD OR BAD? | Competitive Advantage:

05-13 [_] A Person's Goals should not be to Glorify himself: beCause that is for the Purpose of Vanity and Pride, which is almost Guaranteed to Produce Negative Effects, if not Death: beCause Pride comes before Destruction, as King Solomon Warned, in *Proverbs 16:18*. †§‡

Through competitions students can gain better understanding of how to deal with conflicting opinions and ideas. They can learn how to collaborate with widely differing personalities. They can learn to manage subjectivity in their lives. And they can learn to better gauge and evaluate risks. Jul 4, 2016

www.competitionsciences.org › 2016/07/04 › 10-ways-co...
10 Ways Competitions Enhance Learning | Institute of Competition

05-14 [_] See: https://youtu.be/CaELQS5kTso New Money: The Greatest Wealth Creation Event in History, if you want to See what Competition does for People.

Competition teaches commitment.

Children **will** learn how to commit to important events by being involved in sports through weekly schedules. Organized sports **teach** kids how to be disciplined during practice, how to focus on the task, and how to have patience. Jan 4, 2016

allgymnastics.com › blogs › parents › benefits-competition
Benefits of Competition - AllGymnastics.com

Why is increased competition bad?

Because economic **competition** can be hard on businesses, it may harm companies you regularly support. ... Free market **competition** can also lead to monopolies, with the biggest players dominating the market and ultimately leading to fewer, lower quality choices.

bizfluent.com › info-8455003-advantages-disadvantages-...
What Are the Advantages & Disadvantages of Economic Competition?

05-15 [_] How is a Poor Person with a Great Idea going to Compete with a Huge Corporation, which has Billions of Dollars to Invest in some Cheap Trash to Sell?

What is competition and why is it important?

It creates jobs and provides people with a choice of employers and work places. **Competition** also reduces the need for governmental interference through regulation of business. A free market that is competitive benefits consumers- and, society and preserves personal freedoms.

ago.mo.gov › civil-division › consumer › antitrust-laws
The Importance of Competition - Missouri Attorney General

05-16 [_] Meanwhile, the Masses of People in this World of Woes go without the Basic Necessities of LIFE, without Fresh Clean Air to Breathe, without Pure Living Water to Drink, Cook with, and Shower themselves in; without Wholesome Natural Foods to Eat, without Natural Clothing to Wear, and without Secure Houses to Liv within, within those **"GLORIOUS Swanky Hotels Castles and Fortresses!"** **(Beautiful Planned City States for WISE Intelligent Well-Educated People with Common Sense and Good Understanding!) By The Worldwide People's Revolution!® Book 019B**, which they never even Heard of: beCause, WHO could Afford to Advertise them? Who would Believe in them, even if they Heard an Advertisement for them? Just the Sound of "Fortress" Spooks them Away: beCause they Conjure up Visions of Medieval Castles, which have no Connection nor Relationship with God's Swanky Fortresses. ‡

What is a competitive person like?

If you're **competitive**, you **want** to be the best. No one **likes** to lose, but if you are a **competitive person**, it will be especially disappointing to see someone else win. People who are **competitive like** to compete — to find out who knows the most, runs the fastest, can eat the most hot dogs, and so on.

www.vocabulary.com › dictionary › competitive
competitive - Dictionary Definition : Vocabulary.com

05-17 [_] In the Swanky Fortress System, everyone is a Winner, including the most Poorest of Creatures of all Races and Nations, who only have to Contribute their 4 Hours of Common Skilled Labor per Workday, unless they are too Old to Work, in which Cases they will be Cared for by: **"The Swanky Association of Compassionate Caretakers!"** — who will be Supported by the Voluntary Tithes and Freewill Offerings of: **"The Swanky Associations of Working Soldiers!" (A Fascinating Collection of Various Kinds of Voluntary Working Soldiers!) By The Worldwide People's Revolution!®** Book 018B. After all, what is the Cost of an Extra Bed in one of those Billion-dollar "Beautiful Swanky Stone Dome Home COMPLEXES!" (HOW to Build SECURE Tax-proof, Insurance-proof, Self-air-conditioned, Paint-proof, Rot-proof, Termite-proof, Mouse-proof, Fireproof, Tornado-proof, Hurricane-proof, Thief-proof, and BOMB-PROOF Houses!) By The Worldwide People's Revolution!® Book 102?

How do you deal with being too competitive?

To stop **being so competitive**, try working through the emotions behind it. You can also work on your own self-esteem and try to learn how to celebrate successes in yourself and others. Apr 26, 2020

www.wikihow.com › Stop-Being-Competitive
3 Ways to Stop Being Competitive - wikiHow

Being **competitive** can have an ugly connotation in our society. It has become, in some ways, synonymous with greed, envy and narcissism. But feeling **competitive** isn't always about climbing the ladder, winning the race or getting ahead. **Competitive** feelings are completely natural. Sep 10, 2013

www.psychologytoday.com › blog › compassion-matters
The Benefits of Feeling Competitive | Psychology Today

05-18 [_] ♦ Even a Cabbage Plant will Compete with the other Cabbage Plants for Moisture and Nourishment in the Topsoil; but, I have never known a Cabbage Plant that Destroyed all of the other Cabbage Plants in the Garden, just to Prosper, have you?

Is too much competition bad for students?

However, **too much competition** can also cause us to crack and deters our success. When the **competition is too** high, we over-work ourselves by adding in extracurricular activities to fill our resumes, we take challenging classes so that our transcripts look good.

wfuogb.com › 2016/04 › competition-is-healthy-but-too-...
Competition is healthy, but too much is detrimental

05-19 [_] When you are Attending to your Cabbage Plants, Watermelons, Cantaloupes, Tomatoes, Cucumbers, Carrots, Onions, Potatoes, Sweet Corn, Okra, Kale, Cauliflower, Broccoli, Squashes, or whatever you have in your Garden, you could Pretend that you are Competing with your Naaberz, who also have their own Plants to Care for; and therefore, you might Want to make Sure that you Follow "The LUSCIOUS All-Mineral Organic Method of Gardening!" (HOW to Grow DELICIOUS Satisfying Foods for Potential Kingz and Kweenz in Beautiful Swanky PALACES!) By The Worldwide People's Revolution!® Book 021B, which is a Companion Book of: "Orgimmick Gardening at its Best!" (HOW to Grow Delicious Satisfying Foods without a 10-Million-Dollar Investment!) By The Worldwide People's Revolution!® Book 079, whereby you will be Hard-pressed to Do Better than our Selected King has already Done, who

Holds World Records; but, not beCause of Trying to Compete with anyone: beCause he never did that. In Fact, those Sweet Mild Green Onions were the Best in the Whole World, which were 3-feet Tall, with an Extra-Good Flavor, like something from *the Garden of Eden,* itself! †§‡

Why competition is bad for education? ⌃

Competition can be **negative** when it leads to unbalanced living or forces students to give up their other interests. Parents and teachers can encourage students to have a balanced approach to preparing and executing academic challenges, without sacrificing their other passions. Jun 25, 2018

www.theclassroom.com › positive-negative-effects-compe…
Positive & Negative Effects of Competition on Academic Achievement

05-20 [_] ♦ A Student might Prefer to Help those **"Seven Great Armies of Working Soldiers!" (HOW to Provide a Way for Everyone to WORK: so as to Eliminate Poverty, Crimes, Drug Abuses, Prisons and Unnecessary Taxes!) By The Worldwide People's Revolution!® Book 015B, to Build his:** "Beautiful Swanky Stone Dome Home COMPLEXES!" (HOW to Build SECURE Tax-proof, Insurance-proof, Self-air-conditioned, Paint-proof, Rot-proof, Termite-proof, Mouse-proof, Fireproof, Tornado-proof, Hurricane-proof, Thief-proof, and BOMB-PROOF Houses!) By The Worldwide People's Revolution!® Book 102, when he is only 12 Years Old, and Full of Ambition, even as I was, who has no Interest in making himself into an Endless Bills Slave, just to Liv a Good Life. Therefore, I Challenge all Public Schools in the entire World, to Ask their Students (and especially the Boys), if they would not Choose to Check the above Box with a LARGE GREEN-X Mark, rather than Waste the Best Years of their Lives going to "The Public School of IGNERUNT FQLZ!" (HOW we have been GRAATLEE DISEEVD by Capitalism!) By The Worldwide People's Revolution!® Book 024B: beCause they can further their Education after they have Moved Into their "Beautiful Swanky PALACES!" (A New Concept in Living Habits — Swanky Palaces for Poor People!) By The Worldwide People's Revolution!® Book 066. Indeed, they no longer have to Wait for 60 Years, just to Own a Wooden / Plastic Firetrap House to Liv in, when it is Possible and most Practical to Liv in one of those **"GLORIOUS Swanky Hotels Castles and Fortresses!" (Beautiful Planned City States for WISE Intelligent Well-Educated People with Common Sense and Good**

Understanding!) By The Worldwide People's Revolution!® Book 019B, Rent-free! ‡

What are the disadvantages of competitive pricing?   ︿

One **advantage of competitive-**based **pricing** is that it avoids **price competition** that can damage the company. **Disadvantages** include that businesses have to attract customers in other ways, since the **price** will not grab the customer's interest. The **price** may also barely cover production costs, resulting in low profits.

courses.lumenlearning.com › boundless-business › chapter
Pricing Methods | Boundless Business - Lumen Learning

05-21 |_| Competition has made it Possible for Capitalists to Produce Trainloads of Trash, which no one Needed, and no one should have Wanted, while Depriving themselves of the Basic Necessities of LIFE, which everyone Needed, even if they did not get Informed about it, which can easily be Proven in a Courtroom: beCause People were not Born to be Robots, Education Slaves, Work Slaves, Tax Slaves, Insurance Slaves, Interest Slaves, Home-owner Slaves, ElecTrickery Bills Slaves, Food Bills Slaves, Water Bills Slaves, Gas Bills Slaves, Transportation Bills Slaves, Repair Bills Slaves, Entertainment Bills Slaves, Drug Bills Slaves, Doctor Bills Slaves, Hospital Bills Slaves, Childcare Bills Slaves, Nursery Home Bills Slaves, Funeral Home Bills Slaves, nor any other Kind of SLAVES, when it is Possible for all of them to be FREE, Healthy, Wealthy and HAPPY! Yes, it only Requires **"The New RIGHTEOUS One-World Government!" (HOW to Establish a Righteous One-World Government without Going to WAR!) By The Worldwide People's Revolution!® Book 056,** which is a Companion Book of: **"The CONSTITUTION for the New RIGHTEOUS One-World Government!" (HOW all Peoples can get True Justice, and Celebrate the Great Year of JUBILEE!) By The Worldwide People's Revolution!®** Book 016B.

Is competition bad for the economy?   ︿

Free market **competition** can also lead to monopolies, with the biggest players dominating the market and ultimately leading to fewer, lower quality choices. **Economic competition** is a fact of life for any business, but it's clearly not all good or **bad** for anyone.

bizfluent.com › info-8455003-advantages-disadvantages-...
What Are the Advantages & Disadvantages of Economic Competition?

05-22 [_] The Swanky Fortress System Eliminates all of that Business Competition Nonsense: beCause, each Family is Set Up Properly for LIVING, at Home, whereby it does not Matter if they have anything for Sale: beCause they are already Living in one of those "Beautiful Swanky PALACES!" (A New Concept in Living Habits — Swanky Palaces for Poor People!) By The Worldwide People's Revolution!® Book 066, with no Bills. However, if they Want to Occupy their Hands and Minds with the Production of something Special and Beautiful, they are Welcome to Do that. In Fact, they can Invent any Good Thing that they can Think of, and Sell it for a Profit, and use the Money for going on Swanky Vacations to other Swanky Fortresses, whereby they can Buy other Beautiful Things to Fill their Houses with, if they Sincerely Believe that any such things will make them Happy, even though we already Know for a Fact that they will NOT! †§‡

> **Brain** scientists have discovered that acting to improve via **competing** or mastering a new skills alters brainwaves that bolster our performance and our intellectual capabilities. Even the simplest of **competitions** can improve **brain** power. Sep 7, 2019
>
> www.cleverism.com › how-competition-affects-your-brain
> How Competition Affects Your Brain | Cleverism

05-23 [_] If you Want to Discover what True Freedom will Do for Brain Power, just give any Teenage Boy the Necessary Money for Building whatever he might Imagine to be Good, and tell him that there is an Unlimited Supply of that Money, if he can Prove that he Needs it, whereby he will be Wanting to Explore the Inside of Mars! †§‡§§

> **Mars** have a very thin atmosphere. But **moon** do bot have any. **Moon** is only celestial sphere visited by human beings.. **Mars** is the most possible place in solar system where some microbes may be still found in underground caves..
>
> www.quora.com › What-is-the-difference-between-the-m...
> What is the difference between the moon and mars? - Quora

05-24 [_] Notice that the Brain Power of the Person who wrote the above Statement was not Functioning very Well. It should possibly read like this: Mars has a very Thin Atmosphere; but, neither our Moon, nor the Moons of Mars have any Atmospheres. Our Moon is a Celestial Sphere, which has never been Visited by Human Beings: beCause there was no Rocket Launcher on the Moon for Propelling the Lunar Escape Module (LEM) away from the Moon at 4,000 Miles per Hour (MpH), which is more than twice the Speed of a Bullet! In Fact, the LEM had no more than 10 Gallons of Rocketdyne Fuel for Escaping, which is WHY that

NASA Conveniently Lost the Blueprints for the LEM. The Contraption at the far right was supposedly left on the Moon by the AstroNAUGHTIES, who Obviously LIED about Walking on the Moon: beCause of Desperately Wanting to be the FIRST Men on the Moon, which is Proof that Competition is very BAD, if that is the Case, which can be Proven at: "The GREAT Worldwide TELEVISED Court HEARING!" (That Great Meeting of the Most-Intelligent and Well-Educated Minds!) By The Worldwide People's Revolution!® Book 041B, along with the HoloHOAX, the Kennedy Assassination Cover-up, the Waco Texas Cover-up Murder Case, the Oklahoma City Bombing Cover-up Murder Case, and the Evil Events of September 11th, 2001 False Flag Murder Case. †§‡

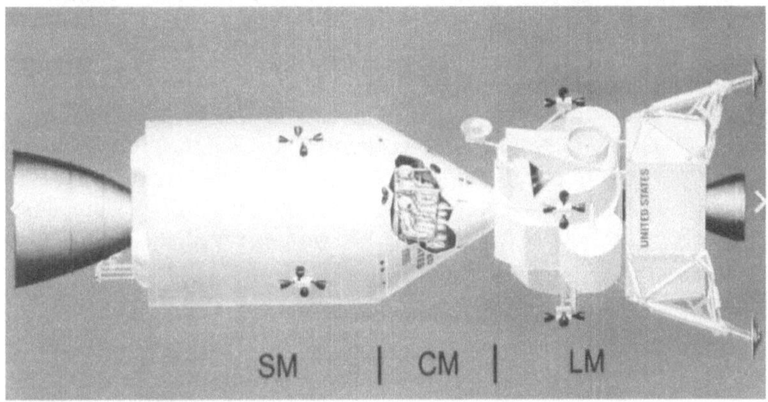

When we are feeling low or less confident about ourselves, we focus our attention on others who we think are doing worse than us in some aspect to make ourselves feel better. So **life is indeed about comparsion and competition.** ... Without **competition** there would be no improvement. Science would not advance as much.

www.quora.com › Is-life-competition
Is life competition? - Quora

05-25 |_| The Person who wrote the above Statement was not very Well-Educated. It should read: When we are Feeling Low, or less Confident about ourselves, we sometimes Focus our Attention on other People, whom we Imagine are doing Worse than we are in some Aspect of Life, in order to make ourselves Feel Better about ourselves. So, Life is in Deed Partly about Comparisons and Competitions. ... without Competition, there might not be any Improvements in Things. Science might not Advance as much, even though it is Doubtful that Science will ever be Able to Improve on the Design and Construction of anything that was Created by the Gods, including the Most-Perfect Human Being, who has yet to be Bred by a Careful Selection of Holy Parents, even as Men Select Special Racehorses to Breed, in Order to get a Winner, which is not a Sin of any Kind: beCause Jehovah God also Wants the Best of Good Healthy Men to Govern this World of Wonders with Jesus Christ, who was Born from a Virgin, who was the Offspring of 2 Holy Parents, who both Fasted and Prayed for 40 Consecutive Nights and 40 Consecutive Days, according to: **"The Proper RULES for FASTING!" (The Complete Instruction Manual for True Repentance!) By The Worldwide People's Revolution!® Book 046,** which is a Companion Book of: **"HOW to Become a HOLY Man!" (40 Good Reasons WHY People Should FAST and PRAY!) By The Worldwide People's Revolution!®** Book 045, which is a Companion Book of: **"The Gospel According to our Elected King!" (The Good News from the Most Modern Perspective!) By The Worldwide People's Revolution!®** Book 077, which is a Companion Book of: **"The New MAGNIFIED Version of The GOOD NEWS According to Saint JOHN!" (The Gospel According to Saint John Zebedee Boanerges [pronounced Boo-an-er-jeez] in Plain English!) By The Worldwide People's Revolution!®** Book 062, which is a Companion Book of: **"The New MAGNIFIED Version of the PSALMS of King David!" (The Understandable Version of the Famous Psalms in Plain English!) By The Worldwide People's Revolution!®** Book 064.

How do you stop viewing your life as a competition?

So my solution is this: Know who you are and know that's enough. You do not have to be someone else, and you do not have to "prove your **life**" to other people. Choose to be your own person, and **stop** treating your **life** like it's a **competition**. "Instead of waiting for someone else to change things, change them yourself." Apr 10, 2018

mollyhostudio.com › blog › how-to-stop-treating-your-lif...
How To Stop Treating Your Life Like A Competition — molly ho

05-26 [_] So, I got to Thinking about that, really HARD, and Concluded that it will Require the United Effort of **"Seven Great Armies of Working Soldiers!" (HOW to Provide a Way for Everyone to WORK: so as to Eliminate Poverty, Crimes, Drug Abuses, Prisons and Unnecessary Taxes!) By The Worldwide People's Revolution!®** Book 015B, just to Accomplish what is Needed for Solving our Massive Problems, beginning with Extreme Poverty among 7-plus Billion Extremely Ignorant People, not to Mention their Countless Crimes, Drug Abuses, and Stuffed Prisons, whose Occupants are Longing to be LIBERATED by **"The Swanky Sword of Divine Truths!" (The Most-**

Powerful Weapon in the Whole Universe!) By The Worldwide People's Revolution!® Book 067. However, I do Agree that, instead of Waiting for God to Change Things, we should get Busy and Change them, ourselves; but, only According to God's Master Plan, and not According to the Plans of Ignorant FOOLS, which is WHY that we, the People, must DEMAND: "The GREAT Worldwide TELEVISED Court HEARING!" (That Great Meeting of the Most-Intelligent and Well-Educated Minds!) By The Worldwide People's Revolution!® Book 041B, whereby we might Learn what God's Plan is! †§‡

Summary of The 8 Ways To Be More Competitive

1. Know The Game Never Ends.

2. Always give 110%

3. Compare Yourself Only To Yourself.

4. Get In Touch With Your Dark Side.

5. Differentiate Yourself.

6. Learn How To Lose.

7. Never Make Excuses.

8. Give Credit When Credit Is Due.

Mar 1, 2020

edlatimore.com › how-to-be-competitive

How to be competitive | Ed Latimore

05-27 [_] It would Require a Book to Explain all of those Things. I am not going to Waste my Time with it. Sorry about that.

A healthy **competitive environment** is **good** for progress both in the field of studies and also in the field of work. However, a **highly competitive environment** is injurious to development and progress both in the field of studies and also in the field of work.
Jun 1, 2019

brainly.in › question

is a highly competitive environment good or bad for studying or ...

05-28 |_| Just Think, my Friend, suppose that 2 or 3 Swanky Fortresses were Competing, to see which one could Produce the most Artistic Baroque Architecture in their Swanky Castles, which might Require 300 to 700 Years to Finish them — who would know WHO Won the Competition? Therefore, just Forget about Competing with anyone, and *"Do with all of your Might whatsoever your Hands Discover to Do, as if Doing it for God, and not for People: beCause God is the only Just Rewarder, who alone can Judge us, who is not so Interested in what we Do to Puff Up our Pride, as he is Interested, and Greatly Concerned with what we Think, and HOW we Act toward one another."* — *The New MAGNIFIED Version in Plain English.*

Healthy competition focuses on delivering a quality product and continuously looking for ways to improve it so that it's better than the **competitors**. Unhealthy **competition** is negative and focuses on pointing out the flaws in the **competing** products.

www.quora.com › How-do-you-define-healthy-competition
How to define healthy competition - Quora

05-29 |_| **"The New RIGHTEOUS One-World Government!" (HOW to Establish a Righteous One-World Government without Going to WAR!) By The Worldwide People's Revolution!® Book 056,** will not be Focusing on Competing with any other Governments: beCause none of them can Compete with a Government that has an Unlimited Supply of Good Money, which must be EARNED by Honest Labor. Indeed, that Good Government will Search the World over for the Most-Intelligent and Well-Educated People, even if they are only Grade School DROPOUTS, who have Discovered HOW to Do something Better than the other People, no matter what it is, who should take the Time to Write their Ideas in Computers, and Save them on Papers: beCause the Whole Earth could be Struck with a Bolt of Lightning that could Destroy all Computers and Electronic Gadgets, Worldwide; and then that Important Information could be Lost, which would be a Tragedy! Therefore, it is Wise to Save that Information in several Ways. Moreover, all Products that are Produced at Swanky Fortresses will be GRADED for their Goodness, which is Explained in: **"The CONSTITUTION for the New RIGHTEOUS One-World Government!" (HOW all Peoples can get True Justice, and Celebrate the Great Year of JUBILEE!) By The Worldwide People's Revolution!® Book 016B.** No Low-grade, Low-class Trash will be Mass-produced at any Swanky Fortresses. Furthermore, Products that are Produced Outside of Swanky Fortresses will be Graded before being Sold within Swanky Forts. ‡

First and foremost **advantage** of **perfect competition** is that chances of consumer exploitation are very low in case of this type of market structure because in **perfect competition** sellers do not have any monopoly pricing power and hence they cannot influence the price of the product or charge higher than the normal price ... Dec 20, 2015

www.letslearnfinance.com › advantages-and-disadvantage...
Advantages and Disadvantages of Perfect Competition

05-30 [_] All Common Tools and Useful Equipment will be Free of Charges at Swanky Fortresses for whomever Lives within them. Outsiders may Buy those Tools, if they Want to. ‡

Is fierce competition a good idea or bad idea? ... **Competition** is healthy because with **competition** not everyone's a winner. **Competition** forces the opposing company to work hard and produce better products. Healthy **competition** results in lower prices for products and better quality for the customers.

sites.google.com › home › philosophical-prompts › ameri...
American Competitive Prompt - English 10 Survival Site - Google

05-31 |_| But, behold, WHERE are those "**GLORIOUS Swanky Hotels Castles and Fortresses!**" (**Beautiful Planned City States for WISE Intelligent Well-Educated People with Common Sense and Good Understanding!**) By The Worldwide People's Revolution!® Book 019B, which would Eliminate the Need for any Dangerous, Polluting, Noisy, Expensive Vehicles for Transportation? Indeed, you are Welcome to Produce your own Swanky Fortress, which might Cost 10 to 300 Trillion Dollars — depending on how Big you plan on making it; but, behold, you do not have the MONEY for Doing it: beCause you are a Poor Ignorant Capitalist, who cannot See the Vision of having "**Seven Great Armies of Working Soldiers!**" (**HOW to Provide a Way for Everyone to WORK: so as to Eliminate Poverty, Crimes, Drug Abuses, Prisons and Unnecessary Taxes!**) By The Worldwide People's Revolution!® Book 015B, in order to Build those Fortresses Correctly, on a Grand Scale, and for everyone who Wants to Liv within them! Indeed, even if a Company can See the Vision of it, it cannot Afford to Build so much as ONE! ‡

What would happen if there was no competition? If there was no competition in the markets, companies woud neglect technological development and cost reduction efforts. Price and service **would** become more advantageous to companies, and consumers **would** result in **no** receipt of benefits.

www.jftc.go.jp › ippan › part1 › demerit
Reasons we are able to buy good quality products at low prices ...

There are four types of competition in a free market system: **perfect competition**, monopolistic competition, oligopoly, and **monopoly**.

2012books.lardbucket.org › books › s05-05-monopolistic...
Monopolistic Competition, Oligopoly, and Monopoly

There are **three** primary **types of competition**: direct, indirect, and replacement **competitors**.

study.com › academy › lesson › what-is-competition-in-m...
What is Competition in Marketing? - Definition & Types - Video ...

Check out the 7 signs you're too competitive...

1. You'll do whatever it takes to win.

2. You take winning a little too seriously. ...

3. People are afraid of you. ...

4. Everything becomes a contest. ...

5. You're constantly comparing yourself to others. ...

6. You love rubbing it in when you win. ...

7. You're a sore loser. ...

People with the **strength** of **Competition** feel they can succeed at something, because they have the ability to assess a given situation, compare the elements at hand, and know with some certainty that they can win. ... Most often, the **strength** of **Competition** is seen when someone is actually **competing** to win.

www.leadershipvisionconsulting.com › how-the-strengths...
How the StrengthsFinder theme of Competition can be Generative

Is competition good for the economy?

Competition from many different companies and individuals through free enterprise and open markets is the basis of the U.S. **economy**. When firms compete with each other, consumers get the best possible prices, quantity, and quality of goods and services. ... One important benefit of **competition** is a boost to innovation.

www.consumer.ftc.gov › games › youarehere › pages › pdf
How Competition Works - Consumer.ftc.gov - Federal Trade ...

05-32 [_] Here are some Examples of what those Americans get. Where are their Gardens?

Panoramic view of the Caracas valley from Parque Nacional El Ávila

Do you See any Gardens? How would they Feed themselves, if the
Rain should Stop?

46% OF D.C.'S POPULATION IS BLACK. IF IT WERE TO BECOME A STATE, D.C. WOULD SURPASS MISSISSIPPI TO HAVE THE LARGEST PROPORTION OF BLACK PEOPLE AMONG ALL STATES.

They are Trying to Sell some of the Capitalist Trash that they have Collected. They call it a "Garage Sale," which is Magnified at "Flea Markets," which sometimes Cover entire City Blocks. Notice that it is a House, which some Poor Person Lived in. What is it Worth? It is the House of an American SLAVE, who Needs to be Liberated by Provable Truths. See: "What is WRong with those CRAZY CHRISTIANS?" (A Self-Examination of the Heart of the Body of Good Government!) By The Worldwide People's Revolution!® Book 076.

How does competition help the economy?

Competition bolsters the productivity and international competitiveness of the business sector and promotes dynamic markets and **economic** growth. ... The most obvious benefit of **competition** is that it results in goods and services being provided to consumers at **competitive** prices. Nov 12, 2002

www.justice.gov › atr › speech › role-competition-promot...
The Role Of Competition In Promoting Dynamic Markets And ...

05-33 [_] For Example, Proper Organic Gardening Costs about 10 Times more to Produce Fruits and Vegetables, than the Chemical Method with Pesticides, Herbicides, and NPK Fertilizers. For Example, Good Rich Well-Watered Topsoil might Grow Weeds and Grasses 4 or 5 Times as Rapidly as Normal Farmland, which Means that the Organic Farmer would have to MOW OFF his Grasses and Weeds several Times during each Growing Season, while the Modern Chemical Farmer would only have to Spray the Ground with Cancer-causing Round*up* one Time per Growing Season. Therefore, the Organic Farmer must do a LOT more Work, at a much-greater Expense. Therefore, how can the Price of his Produce Compete with that of the Chemical Farmer?

5 Benefits of Cooperation

- It fosters peer learning and self-improvement. Working within a team helps us to create an environment which inspires collective knowledge, resources and skills. ...

- Teamwork promotes diversity. ...
- Delegation of task becomes easy. ...
- Teamwork encourages healthy competition. ...
- Increased creativity and innovation.

  Jul 8, 2016

www.psychreg.org › benefits-of-cooperation

5 Benefits of Cooperation | Psychreg

When you engage in a **competition**, and especially when you win, your **brain's** reward system releases a rush of dopamine into your **brain**, resulting in a feeling of pleasure. Sep 7, 2019

www.cleverism.com › how-competition-affects-your-brain

How Competition Affects Your Brain | Cleverism

05-34 |_| Just Think of the Euphoria that would Flood every Mind in the World, after the Completion of the First Glorious Swanky Fortress, which would Greatly Raise the Standard of Living for everyone who gets to Liv within it, by as much as 100 Times! And that would Hopefully Inspire everyone to Want to Build more of them, until everyone gets to Liv within them. ‡

Competition teaches us about goal setting. Creating and setting goals is an important part of being in any competitive landscape. ... Goals created for **competition** contribute to building persistence and determination as individuals increase their challenges and develop a mindset focused for **success**. Nov 25, 2016

leaderonomics.com › necessity-competition-leadership

Why Competition is Necessary for the Leaders of Tomorrow ...

05-35 |_| The Objective should be COOPERATION, not Competition. None of the **Seven Great Armies of Working Soldiers** should be Competing with one another; but, if they Want to, they can Compete with the Outside World, which has already Lost the Contest: beCause of Building Trash Dumps like those thousands of UGLY Cities of

Confusion, which every Sane Person can Agree was a Huge Waste of Time, Money, Materials, and Energy. Indeed, if you Agree, please Check the above Box with a Large Green-X Mark; but, if you Disagree, please Check it with a Large Red-X Mark.

Exploitation of Consumers

Free enterprise allows producers to purposely withhold supply from entering the marketplace, causing consumers to pay higher prices. The system also limits the access that consumers have to suitable alternative products.

www.theclassroom.com › negative-effects-of-free-enterpri...

Negative Effects of Free Enterprise - TheClassroom.com

Disadvantages Of A Free Market Economy

1. Poor Quality. Since profit maximization is the biggest motivation for firms, they may try to reduce their costs unethically. ...
2. Merit Goods. ...
3. Excessive Power of Firms. ...
4. Unemployment and Inequality. ...
5. 4 thoughts on "Free Market"

05-36 [_] Free Enterprise has never Mentioned the Swanky Fortress System. It has never been Voted on. It has never even been Discussed by any Congress. News Reporters are SILENT! Why?

— Chapter 06 —

Will the Church of China Repent?

06-01 [_] If you Watched this Video: https://youtu.be/CaELQS5kTso New Money: The Greatest Wealth Creation Event in History, you are probably Greatly Concerned about the Future of "The Divided States of United Lies!" (The so-called "United States of North America" in Disguise!) By The Worldwide People's Revolution!® Book 058: beCause there is no Way that Americans can Compete with those Ambitious Chinese People, who have Traditionally been very Hardworking Honest People, who Hate Liars — even though they do have some Cheaters among them, who like to Steal Patents: beCause, Capitalism is just a Money Game to them, and all is Fair in Love, War, and Capitalism. However, it Greatly Upsets the American Capitalists, who have Lost Billions of Dollars to those Tricky Chinese, who only became Tricky: beCAUSE of Capitalism. Therefore, they should be the First to Trash it, and Accept the Swanky Fortress System, which can Prosper much more than Capitalism at its Best. For Example, there are no Dangerous Vehicles, no Gasoline-powered Tools within the Finished Fortresses. Therefore, there is Fresh Clean Air at all Times, which all Chinese People will Greatly Appreciate, after Breathing such Bad Air as one might Discover in Beijing, which is the Capital, which should be a Good Example for the Remaining Cities of China, which seems to Trap the Pollution, which is sometimes so THICK that one cannot See a Stop-Light that is only one City Block away! Of course, that also Happens in Lost Angels, Californicate, and other American Cities of Confusion, Worldwide. †§‡

06-02 [_] O Good Pastor of Uncommon Sense, the Chinese People have gone to a LOT of Effort to Build their New Cities, which are more Beautiful than American Cities: beCause they have had the Advantages of Modern Technologies. Therefore, they are the Envy of the World, you might say, even though Honest Chinese People Freely Confess that they would have done much Better for themselves, if they had Built those "GLORIOUS Swanky Hotels Castles and Fortresses!" (Beautiful Planned City States for WISE Intelligent Well-Educated People with Common Sense and Good Understanding!) By The Worldwide People's Revolution!® Book 019B, whereby they could have had a Billion or more Luscious All-Mineral Organic Gardens, with Billions of Fruit Trees, Nut Trees, Grape Vines, Berry Bushes, Flower Gardens, and Spacious Vegetable Gardens with Flavorful Foods to Eat, as Opposed to those Chemical Abominations. Indeed, it is probably their Greatest Regret: beCause, they could have had all of those Good Things, as well as Concert Halls, Theaters, Gymnasiums, Tennis Courts, large Heated Swimming Pools, Bowling Alleys, Ice-skating Rinks, Roller-skating Rinks, Temples, Mosques, Synagogues, Churches, and tens of thousands of those "Royal Swanky Buffets!" (The Best Feasts in the Whole World!) By The Worldwide People's Revolution!® Book 103. Yes, the Possibilities were there, if they had only Consulted your Selected King, before Doing anything; but, they Obviously never Heard of him, even as most of them have never Heard the Teachings of Jesus Christ: beCause they are not Christianized, like the Western Societies. Nevertheless, Chinese are Open-minded People, who will Cheerfully Accept whatever is Proven to be True at, "The GREAT Worldwide TELEVISED Court HEARING!" (That Great Meeting of the Most-Intelligent and Well-Educated Minds!) By The Worldwide People's Revolution!® Book 041B: beCause they are very Logical People, by Nature, who Know in their Hearts that Swanky Fortresses are Far Superior in all Ways for Good Self-defense, and especially in this Nuclear Age. †§‡

06-03 [_] Well, my Friend, it is Sad that the Chinese did not Consult with our Selected King, before they got so Ambitious: beCause they could have all been Moderately Rich, by now. Nevertheless, they can still Repent, and Change their Ways of Living, and get Back to the Land, where they Belong, and thus, Save themselves from a lot of Unnecessary Troubles — such as American Sicknesses and Diseases. However, there is the Pride Problem, now that they have Proven themselves to be Great Competitors, who Played the Capitalist Game Better than Americans Played it, and Beat them at their own Evil Game, you might say. Therefore, that Pride could easily Blind their Minds, whereby they might not even See the Vision of Swanky Fortresses, which they might Imagine is going BACKWARDS, instead of Forward. However, there is nothing Backwards about Picking Sweet Juicy Fruits from Trees, which do not Like Acid Rains, Pollution, Chemical Poisons, nor anything that Capitalism has to Offer on the Altar of Greed and Selfishness. †§‡§§

06-04 [_] O Good Pastor of Uncommon Sense, China has lots of Marble to Work with, and they can all be Living within those "Beautiful Swanky PALACES!" (A New Concept in Living Habits — Swanky Palaces for Poor People!) By The Worldwide People's Revolution!® Book 066, if they Want to be. †‡

06-05 [_] Well, my Friend, chances are they will never Hear about those Swanky Fortresses: beCause of being Distracted by other Nonsense. After all, they have their own iPhones, Televisions and Vain Movies. Besides that, they probably Like the Edomite Slavery System, whereby a few of them have gotten Excessively Rich with the False Riches — such as 0.000,001% of them. †§‡

06-06 [_] O Good Pastor of Uncommon Sense, most of China has been made into a Worthless Desert, which can barely Grow a Stem of Grass: beCause of Overgrazing it with Animals. Therefore, they have a Limited Amount of Good Land to use: beCause most of it was Covered Up with Ugly Highways, High-rise Apartments, Shopping Mauls, and Airports. Indeed, they probably Visualized the People of the Whole World coming to See the Great Stone and Mud Wall of China: beCause it is one of the Manmade Wonders of the World. However, when a Humble Nation of Wise People Construct one of those **"GLORIOUS Swanky Hotels Castles and Fortresses!" (Beautiful Planned City States for WISE Intelligent Well-Educated People with Common Sense and Good Understanding!) By The Worldwide People's Revolution!®** Book 019B, all of the Tourists will Flock into it, and not even Remember the Great Wall of China: beCause it will be like a Child's Sand Box, when Compared with Stone Walls that are 200 feet Tall and 100 feet Thick, and a thousand Miles Long, in Great Stone TERRACES, as many as 60 High! Therefore, when the Chinese Leaders come to their Riit Senses, and Realize how Badly that they were Deceived by Capitalism, they will be Ready for **"The Great ATOMIC NIGHTMARE!" (The Saddest Story in World History!) By The Great White Bald Eagle!** Book 099: beCause of RESENTMENT. Yes, they will Team up with those Russians, who Envy Americans for their Great Riches, who are only 140 Trillion Dollars in DEBT to them, which is the American Form of True Prosperity, which they can Discover in: **"What is True PROGRESS???" (Are we Making any True Progress, at all?) By The Worldwide People's Revolution!®** Book 117. †§‡§§

06-07 [_] Well, my Friend, President Tricky Dick Nixon and his Buddy Henry Kiss-assing-ger made a Grave Mistake when they went to China with their Capitalist Lies and Deceptions: beCause Chinese People do not Like to be Lied to, nor Deceived by any Means, and especially when it concerns their Economy, which is now Based on Capitalist Lies: beCause there are Limited Natural Resources to Work with, which those Chinese will Discover, sooner or later, whereby they will be Thoroughly Pissed Off, as they say, and especially when the Trumpeter is Speaking Evil of them.

06-08 [_] O Good Pastor of Uncommon Sense, like most People, the Chinese like to Eat Good Wholesome Natural Foods, as Opposed to American Abominations, which might have 20 to 30 Chemical Poisons in them, which anyone can Discover on the Ingredient Labels, which Fake Foods are Designed for sitting on Grocery Shelves for Months, and even for YEARS! However, the Capitalist Sellers do not have any Warning Signs on those Foods, which might also Require Years for the Body to Digest and Eliminate those Fake Foods, which Accumulate on their Fat Asses, as Donald Trump might say to Mrs. Black Walrus, who only Weighs 450 Pounds, and has as many Diseases as the Ingredient Labels have Preservatives, Flavor Enhancers, and Mysterious Things that not even a Porcupine Lawyer can reed. †§‡§§ {See: **"Did God or Satan Ordain Medical Doctors?" (Ask Huck Finn and/or Nigger Jim: because neither Tom Sawyer nor Judge Thatcher would Know!) By The Worldwide People's Revolution!® Book 022B.**}

06-09 [_] Well, my Friend, Mrs. Black Walrus is likely to be Offended by all such Words, and call it a Hate Crime, or Racist Slur, Insult, or whatever: beCause of not Studying, **"Is America a White Nation with a Black Heart?" (How to Separate Truth from Fiction!) By The Good Pastor of Uncommon Sense!** Book 118. Indeed, there is hardly a Worse Nigger on this Good Earth than President Donald Trump, who Proved it when he Welcomed those Poor Refugees from Central America with Cruelties — such as Sending their Children to far-away Places, never to be Seen again! He Forgot to, *"Do unto others, as you would have others Do unto you,"* as Jesus said. He Forgot to *"Love your Naaberz just as much as you Love yourself."* After all, God can Arrange for Donald Trump's Spirit to be Born in a Black Body in Haiti, the next Time around, if God wants to get some Justice. Otherwise, he could be Born in some Swamp in Bangladesh, or in some other "A-hole Country over there," as he calls them. Indeed, *"It is a Fearful Thing to Fall into the Hands of the Living God."* — *Hebrews 10:31.*

06-10 [_] O Good Pastor of Uncommon Sense, suppose that God Ordained Donald Trump to Destroy America: beCause of her Multitude of Injustices and Sins, while Serving himself and his own Glory, while Using God to Cover his Hypocrisies? Maybe it is God's Way of getting Revenge on him and all of those Hypocritical Americans, who Refuse to Confess that they are Racist Bigots.

♦ — Chapter 07 — ♦

The Deceived Church of Holy Abortions

07-01 [_] I Sent the following E-Mail Letter to:

A-[_] Dear Brother John,

B-[_] Thank you for Hosting the *Washington Journal* today, and for Believing Provable Truths.

C-[_] Representative Mike Johnson Confessed: "there's no perfect answer," referring to the Kuronavirus Problem.

D-[_] You should have put on the Brakes, right there, and said: But, Mr. Lawyer Johnson, you are WRong: beCause there is a Perfect Solution, and the Dimwitcrats have not Discovered it, which will not only Solve the Viirus Problems; but, no less than 5,000 other Democratic Problems.

E-[_] And he would naturally say, "And what might that be? Please Educate me."

F-[_] And you should say, Go to Amazon Books and Search for: "**GLORIOUS Swanky Hotels Castles and Fortresses!**" (**Beautiful Planned City States for WISE Intelligent Well-Educated People with Common Sense and Good Understanding!**) **By The Worldwide People's Revolution!**® Book 019B, which is a Companion Book

69

of: "The Right Design for Living!" (A List of Great Advantages for Building Beautiful Planned City States!) By The Worldwide People's Revolution!® Book 012B, which is a Companion Book of: "The Low Court of Supreme Injustices is Brought to Trial!" (Our Selected King Butts Heads with the United States Supreme Court, with or without their Black Robes of Hypocrisies and Lies!) By The Worldwide People's Revolution!® Book 011B.

G-[ ] And he would naturally say: "But, I am a God-Ordained Congressman, who is far too Busy raising Money for the next Election Deception, whereby I do not have enough Time to read any such Uninspired Books."

H-[ ] And you should say, Well, in that Case, since you Ride such a High Horse, you should "VOTE for The GOAT!" (The New Political Party that has Guaranteed Solutions for our Massive Problems!) By The Worldwide People's Revolution!® Book 109.

I-[ ] And he would say, "But, I have never Heard of the Goat. WHO is the Insane Goat that I should Vote for?"

J-[ ] And you should say, Trust Jesus, and read: "MARK TWAIN Races for the PRESIDENCY with a Landslide VICTORY!" (The 2020 Presidential Candidates Desperately Need Some STRONG Undefeatable

COMPETITION!) By The Worldwide People's Revolution!® Book 033B.

K-[_] And he would say, "But, King Jesus knows that I do not have Time to read such a Long Book."

L-[_] And you should say, Lots of Laughs! — in that Case, you should read "The CONDENSED Version of MARK TWAIN Races for the PRESIDENCY with a Landslide VICTORY!" (The 2020 Presidential Candidates Desperately Need Some STRONG Undefeatable COMPETITION!) By The Worldwide People's Revolution!® Book 033C. Can you not Manage that?

M-[_] And he would say, "Well, maybe. I will have a look at it." However, he does not Sincerely Intend to Study it, as he should: beCause he is only a Puppet Politician, who is in it for the MONEY, who is a Fake Representative of the People, who does not Believe that there are any "Guaranteed Solutions!" (HOW to Solve our Local and Global Problems in the Most-Rational Manner Possible!) By The Worldwide People's Revolution!® Book 080: beCause that is how he was Brainwashed to Believe by the Lying Conniving Edomites, who do not Want the Masses of Ignorant People to Discover any Guaranteed Solutions for anything: beCause that would be a Great Threat to their Great False Economy. However, you Know for a Fact that there are such Solutions: beCause you have read that Exceptionally Good Book, right? But, not with much Faith.

N-[_] Notwithstanding, *"Faith comes by Learning Provable Truths; and all Provable Truths come from God, who is not the Author of Confusion; but, the Author of Guaranteed Solutions."* — *NMV.* Therefore, are you going to take God's Side, or Satan's Side? When are you going to begin to Correct the Spiritual Babies? Indeed, if everyone in the Whole World were Set Up Properly for Living, at HOME, within "Beautiful Swanky Stone Dome Home COMPLEXES!" (HOW to Build SECURE Tax-proof, Insurance-proof, Self-air-conditioned, Paint-proof, Rot-proof, Termite-proof, Mouse-proof, Fireproof, Tornado-proof, Hurricane-proof, Thief-proof, and BOMB-PROOF Houses!) By The Worldwide People's Revolution!® Book 102, they could simply Lock their Doors, and Stay at Home for a Month or so, and the Viirus would simply go Away: beCause it could not Spread. Therefore, that Plan would Kill it, which can be Proven in a Courtroom. †§‡

O-[_] Oh, by the way, there will be more Viirusez during the Future, and much Worse Plagues, for which there is only ONE Guaranteed Solution, which is to Build those "Beautiful Swanky PALACES!" (A New Concept in Living Habits — Swanky Palaces for Poor People!) By The Worldwide People's Revolution!® Book 066: beCause, "All of the Arguments are in Favor of our Selected King, who has Zero Challengers!" (Before you Attend another Election

Deception, you should Carefully Study this Inspired Book with an Honest Open Mind!) By The Worldwide People's Revolution!® Book 085. Therefore, you should Study: "HOW Righteousness can Overcome Wickedness!" (The Triumph of the Soul who Knows God!) By The Enlightened Professor of Common Sense! Book 093. Otherwise, my Friend, you are going to Suffer with "The Great ATOMIC NIGHTMARE!" (The Saddest Story in World History!) By The Great White Bald Eagle! Book 099.

Sincerely, the Honest Observer and Chief Agitator

P-[_] PS — You can read the Remainder of my ABC Letter in some Inspired Book. Most Sane People will Agree with me. All others are simply "Modern Deceived SLAVES!" (10 Simple Steps for Liberating ALL Modern Slaves, Worldwide, Including Yourself!) **By** Liberty and Justice for ALL! Book 113.

07-02 [_] So, O Good Pastor of Uncommon Sense, what is the Remainder of your ABC Letter to John McArdle? Furthermore, did you Receive any Response from him?

07-03 |_| ♦♦ No, my Friend, I did not Receive any Response from John, in spite of Sending more than a Dozen Exceptionally Good E-mail Letters to him, during the past 5 Years, or so: beCause he has an Excuse or 3.

Q-[_] The First Excuse is this: "We Receive far too many E-mail Letters from People, who Listen to the *Washington Journal,* whereby we cannot possibly Respond to all of them," in spite of the Fact that only a few Letters Require any Responses, which we can easily Prove in a Courtroom. Chances are that they Receive less than a Dozen E-mail Letters per Day, if any more than mine, alone: beCause they do not Post any E-mail Address for Viewers to Use. (Go to Contact on C-SPAN, and Discover it for yourself. They used to have it; but, after I Sent a few Letters to them, they Cut it Off. Brian Lamb used to have a Q&A Program, until I Sent to him just one E-mail Letter, which was all Positive Information, which Ended his Q&A Programs. You can find that Letter in some Book. I have Forgotten which one. Sorry about that.) †§‡

R-[_] Second Excuse: "We are Neutral, and do not take Sides with any Particular Political / Religious Party. Therefore, if we Agreed with you, we would not be Living up to our Guidelines, nor Code of *Washington Journal* Conduct," in spite of the Fact that I do not Care whether or not C-SPAN Hosts Agree nor Disagree with me: beCause my Major Concern is whether or not they got my Messages into their Heads, whereby they might Hear my Viewpoints, and thus, be Able to Ask their Viewers and Listeners the Appropriate Questions for making them THINK: beCause most of them cannot Think very Well, Deeply, nor Clearly, who have no "Guaranteed Solutions" for anything, who are Mostly Lost Sheeps in the Darkness of Ignorance, for the Greater Part of them, who are Unemployed, who are often the most Ignorant Americans: beCause the Well-Educated Americans are at WORK, and do not have Time for the Nonsense on C-SPAN, which is WHY that they normally have less than 2,000,000 Viewers, in a Nation with more than 300 Million People.

S-[_] And their Third Excuse is: "We cannot take the Time to Read Aloud any such Long E-mail Letters on the *Washington Journal,* even if they are more Important than the Information in the Snooze Papers — such as *The New York Times, The Wall Street Journeyman, The Washington Compost, The Shitecago Tribune, The Lost Angel's Herald, The San Fransissies' Dispatch, The Dall-ass Tex-ass Braying Donkey,* nor *The Houston Chronicle:* beCause the Information in those E-mail Letters was not Filtered, nor Approved by the United Press Club (UPI), which Manages all of the News Propaganda, which is WHY that we often Cut Off our Callers, and especially if they Mention Bankers, Jews, the HoloHOAX, the Evil Events of September 11th, 2001, False Flag Operation; the Moon Landing HOAX, the Kennedy Assassination Cover-up, the Waco Texas

Massacre Cover-up, the Pearl Harbor False Flag Operation, the Oklahoma City Bombing Covered-up Federal Crime, the Gordan Kahl Murder, nor Howard Zinn's Famous Book, called: **A People's History of the United States,** which should be Banned from Publication: beCause too much Freedom of Speech and of the Press is BAD for our Great False Economy, and is also a Great Threat to our National Security: beCause too many Americans might Believe all such Propagandist Lies, and thus, Want another REVOLUTION, which would not be Approve by the Federal Burden of False Investigators (FBI), nor by the Central Unintelligent Agencies (CIA): beCause they are the most-Innocent Liars and Poisonous Snakes among us!" †§‡§§

T-[_] Time will Prove you to be Correct, O Good Pastor of Uncommon Sense, even if it Requires the Great Day of God's Good Judgment, who must have Recorded all of it. †§‡

U-[_] I Understand that there will be a Great Judgment Day, or else there will be no Justice for anyone; but, how many Millenniums will that Require?

V-[_] Beardless Vice-President Josephine Biden will get it all Straightened Out, once he Squats in the Oval Orifice, in the Little White Outhouse on Pennsylvania Avenue, on the Capital Dunghill, in the District of Chief Criminals, in George Washington's Backyard: beCause he has Zero "Guaranteed Solutions!" (HOW to Solve our Local and Global Problems in the Most-Rational Manner Possible!) By The Worldwide People's Revolution!® Book 080. †§‡§§

W-[_] I am Wondering if Joe Biden is up to the Task of Running "the Greatest Nation on the Whole Earth," which is only 150 Trillion Dollars in DEBT? (It Climbed by 10 Trillion within the past Hour!) Is he just another Ignorant FOOL, or what? WHO is going to Pay Off those Debts? Indeed, we would have to get into another World War, just to Do that. †§‡§§

X-[_] X-number of People cannot Remember how World War 2 left us hundreds of Billions of Dollars in Debt to the Rich Edomite Bankers, who had no Money to Loan, just 2 Weeks before the Fake Congress Declared War on Germany; but, just as soon as they Declared War, those Rich Edomite Bankers suddenly came up with TRILLIONS of Dollars to Loan to both Sides of that Hateful War: beCause they Gained hundreds of Billions of Dollars on their Profitable Loans, which they will be Happy to Do again, whereby Americans can Waste the next 50 Years of their Lives, Paying Off those Greedy Rich Bankers, when they should be Wise, and Obey the Laws of Moses, whose Not-so-Fake God Commanded him to Declare a YEAR of JUBILEE, once every 50 Years, whereby all Debts must be FORGIVEN, and especially all Debts to Rich Bankers! Yes, you can read it for yourself in *Leviticus 25, King James Version,* or in whatever Version you Like: beCause they all read about the same Way, except for *The New MAGNIFIED Version,* which makes it Clear WHO the Chief Bank Robbers are, and WHY that they should all be put OUT of Business! †§‡§§

Y-[_] I am Yearning for the Happy Day when Jesus Christ Returns, and Establishes "The New RIGHTEOUS One-World Government!" (HOW to Establish a Righteous One-World Government without Going to WAR!) By The Worldwide People's Revolution!® Book 056: beCause, there are "101 Good Reasons and Great Advantages for Establishing a Righteous One-World Government!" (Government By the People, Of the People, and For the People!) By The Worldwide People's Revolution!® Book 104. However, no Politicians have ever Studied those Exceptionally Good Books: beCause they are far too Busy Collecting Money for the next Election Deception. †§‡§§

Z-[_] The Great ZEAL of "The Worldwide People's Revolution!" (A Comprehensive Plan for Obtaining Worldwide Law, Order, Obedience, Peace and True Prosperity!) By The Worldwide People's Revolution!® Book 108, will Change all of that, once they are Discovered, who should Study: "HOW to IDENTIFY God's Elected Ones!" (Are YOU one of the Elect?) By The Worldwide People's Revolution!® Book 095.

07-04 [_] What do any of those Things have to do with **The Deceived Church of Holy Abortions**? How could a Woman have a HOLY Abortion, anyway?? Is that not Contradictory in Nature? †§‡

07-05 [_] Well, my Friend, that is Exactly what I was also Thinking — how could an Abortion be HOLY? Would God Approve of it? Well, in the Case of Nineveh, God COMMANDED IT! Imagine that, if you can? Jehovah God Commanded Jonah to go to Nineveh, and tell those People to REPENT, or else Nineveh would be Destroyed. So, Jonah Reluctantly Obeyed, and the King of Nineveh Heard the Good and Bad News, and Commanded all of the People to REPENT, whereby they all Fasted and Prayed for the next 40 Nights and 40 Consecutive Days, which Jesus called "True Repentance," which it was, which we can Prove in a Courtroom, if anyone is Interested in Provable Truths. †§‡

Dictionary

Search for a word

 **re·pent**
/rəˈpent/

verb

feel or express sincere regret or remorse about one's wrongdoing or sin.
"the priest urged his listeners to repent"

Similar: feel remorse for   **regret**   be sorry for   **rue**   repro

- view or think of (an action or omission) with deep regret or remorse.
  "Marian came to repent her hasty judgment"

- ARCHAIC
  feel regret or penitence about.
  "I repent me of all I did"

What does it mean to repent biblically? ∧

The doctrine of **repentance** as taught in the Bible is a call to persons to make a radical turn from one way of life to another. The **repentance** (metanoia) called for throughout the Bible is a summons to a personal, absolute and ultimate unconditional surrender to God as Sovereign.

en.wikipedia.org › wiki › Repentance
Repentance - Wikipedia

In the Greek language, the word **repent** is metanoia which literally **means** 'to perceive afterwards'. It implies that we can see the consequences of our actions before we act. ... **Repent means** to be very observant, acutely aware. This level of awareness applies to our speech, our emotions, and our intentions. Jan 25, 2016

www.huffpost.com › entry › the-bible-unlocked-what-d_...
The Bible Unlocked: What Does it Really Mean to Repent? |

Repent normally, but tell God you **will** try to ease out of it. ... Forgiveness is an act of grace from God. If you're unable to forgive **someone**, pray to God and ask Him to give you the strength to forgive. Be humble and open your heart to Him; as **people** who have received God's forgiveness, we **should** forgive others.

www.wikihow.com › Repent

How to Repent (with Pictures) - wikiHow

What did Jesus mean by repent?

testifying both to Jews and to Greeks of **repentance** toward God and of faith in our Lord **Jesus Christ**." ... When **Jesus** said "**Repent**," He was talking about a change of heart toward sin, the world, and God; an inner change that gives rise to new ways of living that exalt **Christ** and give evidence of the truth of the gospel. Sep 24, 2015

www.journal-advocate.com › 2015/09/24 › jesus-says-rep...

Jesus says, 'Repent and believe!' – Sterling Journal-Advocate

Why is it important to repent your sins?

In Isaiah 55:7, **the** Bible states that **repentance** brings pardon and forgiveness of **sin**. Apart from **repentance**, no other activities, such as sacrifices or religious ceremonies can secure pardon and forgiveness of **sin**.

en.wikipedia.org › wiki › Repentance

Repentance - Wikipedia

How do I know if I have true repentance?

They are sincere about getting free from sin and aren't justifying or arguing their case any longer. They are **genuine** and sincere about being more Christ-like. -*- Second, they want to clear themselves. This isn't paying for their own sin, they don't want to hide their sin but have it removed at all costs. Jul 12, 2013

www.pbcommercial.com › article › LIFESTYLE

7 Signs of true repentance - Lifestyle - Pine Bluff Commercial - Pine

What is the greatest sin against God?

The unpardonable **sin** is blasphemy **against** the Holy Spirit. Blasphemy includes ridicule and attributing the works of the Holy Spirit to the devil. According to Billy Graham, refusing to turn to **God** and accept his forgiveness is the eternal **sin**.

en.wikipedia.org › wiki › Eternal_sin

Eternal sin - Wikipedia

(The Unholy Church of Graceful Sinners, who are Mostly just Liars and Hypocrites!)

How do you repent for prayer?

Dear Lord Jesus, I know that I am a sinner, and I ask for Your forgiveness. I believe You died for my sins and rose from the dead. I turn from my sins and invite You to come into my heart and life. I want to trust and follow You as my Lord and Savior.

Sinner's prayer - Wikipedia

What are the four steps of repentance?

The first is responsibility: We must recognize that we have done wrong. The second is regret: We must have true remorse for doing wrong and for the pain and problems we've caused. The third is resolve: We must be committed never to repeat the act regardless of the temptations or situation. May 10, 1998

4 STEPS TO REPENTANCE - Chicago Tribune

Who said Repent for the kingdom of God is near?

In the King James Version of the Bible the text reads: "And saying, **Repent** ye, for the **kingdom** of heaven is **at hand**." The New International Version translates the passage as: "and saying, "**Repent, for the kingdom** of heaven is **near**." For a collection of other versions see BibleHub Matthew 3:2.

Matthew 3:2 - Wikipedia

What is blasphemy against the Holy Spirit?

"**Blasphemy against the Holy Spirit**" is conscious and hardened opposition to the truth, "because the **Spirit** is truth" (1 John 5:6). Conscious and hardened resistance to the truth leads man away from humility and repentance, and without repentance there can be no forgiveness.

Eternal sin - Wikipedia

Is repentance a condition of salvation?

In this article we wish to show that **repentance** is also a **condition** to **salvation**. For **repentance** to be a **condition** it would mean that God required one to **repent** in order to be saved from their sins. Sep 27, 2019

Repentance, a condition of salvation | Sampson Independent

What sins does God not forgive?

Biblical passages

Matthew 12:30-32: "Whoever is **not** with me is against me, and whoever **does not** gather with me scatters. And so I tell you, any **sin** and blasphemy **can** be **forgiven**. But blasphemy against the Spirit will **not** be **forgiven**.

en.wikipedia.org › wiki › Eternal_sin
Eternal sin - Wikipedia

Abrahamic religion. The doctrine of **repentance** as taught in the Bible is a call to persons to make a radical turn from one way of life to another. The **repentance** (metanoia) called for throughout the Bible is a summons to a personal, absolute and ultimate unconditional surrender to **God** as Sovereign.

en.wikipedia.org › wiki › Repentance
Repentance - Wikipedia

Does God forgive sins without confession?

However, as **God's** mercy and **forgiveness** is not bound by the Sacrament of Penance, under extraordinary circumstances a mortal **sin can** be remitted through perfect contrition, which is a human act that arises from a person's love of **God**.

en.wikipedia.org › wiki › Mortal_sin
Mortal sin - Wikipedia

A mortal **sin** (Latin: peccatum mortale), in Catholic theology, is a gravely sinful act, which can lead to damnation if a person does not repent of the **sin** before death. ... The **sin** against the Holy Ghost and the **sins** that cry to Heaven for vengeance are considered especially **serious**.

en.wikipedia.org › wiki › Mortal_sin
Mortal sin - Wikipedia

What is the deadliest sin?

Lust, envy, anger, greed, gluttony and **sloth** are all bad, the sages say, but pride is the deadliest of all, the root of all evil, and the beginning of sin. Feb 13, 2006

www.npr.org › templates › story › story
The Seven Deadly Sins: Pride : NPR

What are the 8 Deadly Sins?

- Gula (gluttony)
- Luxuria/Fornicatio (lust, fornication)
- Avaritia (avarice/greed)
- Superbia (pride, hubris)
- Tristitia (sorrow/despair/despondency)
- Ira (wrath)
- Vanagloria (vainglory)
- Acedia (sloth)

en.wikipedia.org › wiki › Seven_deadly_sins

Seven deadly sins - Wikipedia

What does God say about repentance?

When Jesus **said** "**Repent**," He was talking about a change of heart toward sin, the world, and **God**; an inner change that gives rise to new ways of living that exalt Christ and give evidence of the truth of the gospel. Sep 24, 2015

www.journal-advocate.com › 2015/09/24 › jesus-says-rep…

Jesus says, 'Repent and believe!' – Sterling Journal-Advocate

Can you repent without the Holy Spirit?

All sins shall be forgiven, except the sin against the **Holy Ghost**; for Jesus **will** save all except the sons of perdition. ... After a man has sinned against the **Holy Ghost**, there is no **repentance** for him.

en.wikipedia.org › wiki › Eternal_sin

Eternal sin - Wikipedia

Can there be forgiveness without repentance?

Because **there** is no **repentance**. For **forgiveness** to happen, **repentance** must take place. Jun 21, 2015

getpocket.com › ...
Charleston: Forgiveness without Repentance? - Reformation 21

To **repent**, you need to confess your sins to the Lord. Then seek forgiveness from those you have wronged, and restore as far as possible what has been damaged by your actions.

www.churchofjesuschrist.org › for-the-strength-of-youth
Repentance - The Church of Jesus Christ of Latter-day Saints

Is being lazy a sin?

Sloth is one of the seven capital **sins** in Christian teachings. It is the most difficult **sin** to define and credit as **sin**, since it refers to a jumble of notions, dating from antiquity and including mental, spiritual, pathological, and physical states. One definition is a habitual disinclination to exertion, or **laziness**.

en.wikipedia.org › wiki › Sloth_(deadly_sin)
Sloth (deadly sin) - Wikipedia

Is all sin equal in the Bible?

All Sin is not the Same

In fact, the Book of Proverbs (6:16-19) identifies seven things that God hates although there is not any punishment proscribed for those. **Scripture** clearly indicates that God does view **sin** differently and that He proscribed a different punishment for **sin** depending upon its severity. Dec 11, 2014

www.gcu.edu › blog › theology-ministry › all-sin-equal-g...
Is All Sin Equal in God's View? | GCU Blogs - Grand Canyon University

How do you repent in the Bible?

"Rend your heart, and not your garments, and turn unto the Lord your God: for he is gracious and full of compassion, slow to anger and plenteous in mercy, and repenteth him of the evil". In Isaiah 55:7, the **Bible** states that **repentance** brings pardon and forgiveness of sin.

en.wikipedia.org › wiki › Repentance
Repentance - Wikipedia

(The Unholy Church of Graceful Sinners, who are Mostly just Liars and Hypocrites!)

What does the Bible say about turning from your wicked ways?

If **my** people, which are called by **my** name, shall humble themselves, pray and seek **my** face and **turn from their wicked ways**, then I will hear from heaven, and will heal **their** land. Jan 19, 2017

www.governing.com › gov-phil-bryant
If my people, which are called by my name, shall humble themselves ...

What does it mean to repent and believe?

Mark 1:15 records the inspired summary of Jesus' message as He began His ministry: "The time is fulfilled, and the kingdom of God is at hand; **repent and believe** in the gospel." **Repentance** and faith go together because if you **believe** that Jesus is the Lord Who saves (faith), you have a changed mind about your sin and ... Sep 24, 2015

www.journal-advocate.com › 2015/09/24 › jesus-says-rep...
Jesus says, 'Repent and believe!' – Sterling Journal-Advocate

What mean born again?

Born again, or to experience the new birth, is a phrase, particularly in evangelicalism, that refers to "spiritual rebirth", or a regeneration of the human spirit from the Holy Spirit, contrasted with physical birth.

en.wikipedia.org › wiki › Born_again
Born again - Wikipedia

Can apostates be restored?

Certain **apostates** became worse than they were before they believed and **will** suffer eternal death even though they had fully known God. Nevertheless, most people, whether **apostates** or fallen ministers, have an opportunity to repent and be **restored** (Sim.

en.wikipedia.org › wiki › Apostasy_in_Christianity
Apostasy in Christianity - Wikipedia

Are sins forgiven after confession?

While private **confession** of all grave **sins** is now required, **confession** of venial **sins** is recommended but not required. ... If the penitent forget to **confess** a mortal **sin** in **Confession**, the sacrament is valid and their **sins** are **forgiven**, but he must tell the mortal **sin** in the next **Confession** if it again comes to his mind.

en.wikipedia.org › wiki › Sacrament_of_Penance
Sacrament of Penance - Wikipedia

Can all sins be forgiven Catholic?

All sins shall be **forgiven**, except the **sin** against the Holy Ghost; for Jesus **will** save **all** except the sons of perdition. What must a man do to commit the unpardonable **sin**? He must receive the Holy Ghost, have the heavens opened unto him, and know God, and then **sin** against him.

en.wikipedia.org › wiki › Eternal_sin

Eternal sin - Wikipedia

Why is gluttony a sin?

In Christianity, it is considered a **sin** if the excessive desire for food causes it to be withheld from the needy. Some Christian denominations consider **gluttony** one of the seven deadly **sins.**

en.wikipedia.org › wiki › Gluttony

Gluttony - Wikipedia

What are examples of venial sins?

For **example**, someone who tells so-called white lies commits **venial sin**, but if he does it long enough, it's much easier for him to be tempted to tell a big lie later on that would in fact be a mortal **sin**, such as cheating on a test or on his income tax return.

www.dummies.com › religion › christianity › catholicism

Mortal and Venial Sins in the Catholic Church - dummies

What makes a sin venial?

Definition. According to the Catechism of the Catholic Church: 1862 One commits **venial sin** when, in a less serious matter, he does not observe the standard prescribed by the moral law, or when he disobeys the moral law in a grave matter, but without full knowledge or without complete consent.

en.wikipedia.org › wiki › Venial_sin

Venial sin - Wikipedia

Is the F word a mortal sin?

If a **word** refers to a body part, bodily function, or a demeaning way of describing a person, it's this, not profanity. Highly context dependent, but probably venial unless used in wrath, or to deliberately dishonor one's parents, or some other **sin**. Jan 1, 2020

www.reddit.com › Catholicism › comments › is_using_pr...

Is using profanity a venial or mortal sin? : Catholicism - Reddit

What are common mortal sins?

They join the long-standing evils of lust, gluttony, avarice, sloth, anger, envy and pride as **mortal sins** - the gravest kind, which threaten the soul with eternal damnation unless absolved before death through confession or penitence. Mar 11, 2008

www.theage.com.au › world
List of mortal sins gets longer under Vatican overhaul - The Age

Is touching yourself a mortal sin?

In his encyclical, he writes: "In order to be able to grasp the object of an act which specifies that act morally, it is therefore necessary to place oneself in the perspective of the acting person." Masturbation not always incurs grave **sin**, or **mortal sin**, but it can not be said that masturbation is not "gravely wrong" ...

en.wikipedia.org › wiki › Religious_views_on_masturbati...
Religious views on masturbation - Wikipedia

07-06 [_] Now, as you can See, the People who were Asking Mr. Google the Questions were not Exactly Well-Educated, which was no doubt WHY that they were Asking their Questions, to begin with; but, did Mr. Google come up with the Correct Answers?

Can Catholics use condoms?

The **Catholic** ban on the **use** of **condoms**, or any other device, for contraceptive purposes remains. One of the pope's most senior officials, Cardinal Rino Fisichella, told the press conference **condoms** were "intrinsically an evil". Nov 23, 2010

www.theguardian.com › world › nov › catholic-church-c...
Catholic church tries to clear confusion over condom use | World ...

07-07 [_] ♦♦♦♦♦♦♦ For Example, the Question should have been: Do Good Catholics use Condoms? Or, Do Good Christians use Condoms? Answer: NO, they have no Need for them: beCause they Believe in Abortions! HUMBUG! But, God Believes in Abortions, which was Proven in *the Book of Jonah,* where God Commanded the Mothers to Abort their Babies! Indeed, it clearly states that ALL of the People and Animals of Nineveh REPENTED, by Fasting for 40 Nights and 40 Days, which is Guaranteed to Abort any Unborn Babies. Therefore, a City of 120,000 People is Bound to have X-number of Pregnant Mothers within it, who ALL Aborted their Babies, Legally: beCause God Commanded it! Therefore, it is Possible to have a Holy Abortion! Prove me to be WRong, if you can; but, according to the *Scriptures,* you cannot Prove me to be WRong: beCause it is made Perfectly Clear that ALL of the

People of Nineveh REPENTED, while sitting in Ashes, while Covered with Sackcloth. Deny it, and you will go Straight to HELL, you Lying Son of Satan! Jesus Confirmed it in *Matthew 12:41,* saying: *"The men of Nineveh shall rise in judgment with this generation, and shall condemn it: because they repented at the preaching of Jonas; and, behold, a greater than Jonas is here."* — *KJV.* However, just to Clarify it, let me Quote to you *The New MAGNIFY Version (NMV),* which pulls no Punches, which Strikes at the Heart of the American Problems: beCause, the Normal Professing "Christian" has no Idea what it MEANS to REPENT! In Fact, not even the Rev. Dr. Billy Graham had any Idea what it Means: beCause it is not Tawt in Seminary Theological Schools, nor by Mainstream "Evangelicals," like Billy Graham, who was Totally DECEIVED by his own Ignorance concerning that Most-Important-of-ALL Subjects, which is what makes this Inspired Book so VERY Important! Indeed, if what I Teach is the Pure Unadulterated TRUTH, then ALL of those False Religions are WRong! Therefore, Dig the Wax of Unbelief OUT of your Spiritual Ears, and Listen Intently to me: beCause I am not Lying to you, nor being Sarcastic about it. Jesus was Correct — the People of Nineveh Truly Repented, and they did that by Fasting and Praying for Forgiveness for 40 Days, just as it is Written in Gold Lettering in the Temple of GOD, in Heaven: beCause there is no other Way to get RID of Dietary Sins! However, you are Welcome to LIE to yourself about it, and Suffer the Consequences of Dietary Sins! Only YOU will Suffer for it, not me: beCause I am Free! †§‡

07-08 [_] O Good Pastor of Uncommon Sense, I See what you Mean — those Beautiful Ladies would have to REPENT, according to: "The Proper RULES for FASTING!" (The Complete Instruction Manual for True Repentance!) By The Worldwide People's Revolution!® Book 046, just to get Rid of the Accumulated Filth within their Bodies, who are Actually in pretty Good Shape, when Compared with Gluttons and Drunkards that I have Seen, who might Weigh more than twice as much as they Weigh, and not even be Aware that they have Committed any Dietary Sins: beCause the Irreverent LOUDMOUTH Sloth-gut Windbag Hole-in-his-Head never Mentioned those Words in any of his False Sermons: beCause of being another Selfish HOG, himself! Yes, his Primary Motive for Preaching his Worthless Sermons was to get MONEY, Popularity, and Fame — not to Save Sinners from ALL of their Sins: beCause, if those Sinners were Actually SAVED from all of their Sins, they would have no Use for any Stinking Cigarettes, Chewing Tobacco, Curse Words, Dirty Jokes, Fornication, Adultery, Gluttony, Drunkenness, Sodomy, nor SLAVERY. Indeed, they would not be Seeking to Justify ANY Sins, at all, including Education Slavery, Work Slavery, Tax Slavery, Insurance Slavery, Rent Slavery, ElecTrickery Bills Slavery, Food Bills Slavery, Water Bills Slavery, Home-owner Bills Slavery, Interest Bills Slavery, Mortgage Bills Slavery, Gas Bills Slavery, Transportation Bills Slavery, Repair Bills

Slavery, Telephone Bills Slavery, Entertainment Bills Slavery, Internet Bills Slavery, Drug Bills Slavery, Doctor Bills Slavery, Hospital Bills Slavery, Childcare Bills Slavery, Nursing Home Bills Slavery, Funeral Home Bills Slavery, nor any other Kind of SLAVERY, while Singing: ♫ *"I'm so PROUD to be an American, where at least I Know for a Fact that I am Free to Pay all of my Endless Bills, and Consume all of my Countless Pills: beCause, I am Basically just another Ignorant Modern DECEIVED SLAVE!"* {See: **"Was Billy Graham Greatly Deceived?" (Giving Honor to whom Honor is Due!) By The Worldwide People's Revolution!**® Book 083.}

07-09 [_] Well, my Friend, you left Out an Entire List of Evil Things, which True Christians have no Use for, including Candies, Cakes, Pies, Iced-creams, Cookies, Cokes, Lard, Fats, Unnatural Cooking Oils, certain Spices, Pork, Unclean Fishes, Unclean Animals, and whatever Saint Peter Refused to Eat in *Acts 10:* beCause those were Truly Unholy Things for True Christians to EAT, who must be Above the Slime Pits of Egypt. However, most Professing "Christians" use the Vision of Saint Peter to Justify the Eating of Old Dead Rotting Carcasses of Skunks, Snakes, Buzzards, Crows, Magpies, Slugs, Snails, Scorpions, Mice, Rats, Armadillos, Rabbits, Opossums, Raccoons, and whatever they like to Eat: beCause they like to TWIST the *Scriptures* unto their own Damnation, which is Okay: beCause, God only Wants the Best of Honest MEN in his Holy Kingdom, which has none of those Unclean Things in it! However, do not let it Bother your Conscience any Amount: beCause there are DEGREES of Holiness, and also Different Positions of Authority in the Holy Kingdom of All that is GOOD. Therefore, if you only get the Position of a Mop Boy, be Thankful for it: beCause, it is much Better to be a Mop Boy in the Kingdom or Government of God, than to be Cast into an Evil Place like the Lake of Fire, which Burns with Stinking Sulfur, and Smells like Rotten Eggs! Indeed, such an Unholy Place is Prepared for Liars and Hypocritters, like Donald Jaywalking Trump, who could also Repent, if he were Humble Enough to Do so; but, his Pride would never Allow him to Confess his Multitude of Sins, which he Seeks to Justify: beCause he is Obviously a Son of SATAN! But, not to Worry too much for him: beCause he will still Enter into the Kingdom of God before that Murderous George Warmonger Bush and Little Dick Chicanery: beCause, they are even more Deceived than Donald! Nevertheless, the Bottom Line is this: NO UNCLEAN THING WILL ENTER INTO THE HOLY KINGDOM of ALL THAT IS GOOD! Therefore, you must Judge for yourself what is Good for you to Eat and Drink: beCause your Body is supposed to be the Temple of GOD — not the Temple of Swine Eaters, Rapists, Sodomites, Fornicators,

Adulterers, Crotch-grabbers, Baby Abusers, Greedy Selfish Hogs, Murderers, Warmongers, Cruel Masters, Abusive Brutal Policemen, Mutilating Medical Doctors, Lying Preachers, Propagandist School Teachers, Tricky Scientists, nor any other Evil Kind of Creature, who will all be Judged According to their Words and Deeds!

07-10 |_| Therefore, Listen Carefully. The Humble Honest Men of Ancient Nineveh will Arise during the Day of Judgment with this Generation of Evil Doers, and will Condemn it: beCause they Repented According to the Preaching of Jonah, which you can Discover in an Inspired Book, called: "The Gospel According to our Elected King!" (The Good News from the Most Modern Perspective!) By The Worldwide People's Revolution!® Book 077, which was Written by the Spirit of Inspiration, which you dare not Mock nor Ridicule Unjustly, lest you should Spend an Eternity of Torments with other Mockers and Scoffers, who Reject Provable Truths without any Justifiable Causes. After all, *the Book of Jonah,* which consists of just a few short Chapters, can easily be "Red" in just one Hour, or 2, and be Understood as Jesus Understood it, who Accepted it Literally, who also went into the Wilderness, and Fasted for 40 Nights and 40 Days, according to *Matthew 4,* which is Confirmed by other *Scriptures,* which only makes Perfect Sense when you Practice Fasting, yourself, which Requires Time, Patience, Persistence, and OBEDIENCE: beCause it is Possible to Kill yourself by Disobeying "The Proper RULES for FASTING!" (The Complete Instruction Manual for True Repentance!) By The Worldwide People's Revolution!® Book 046. Therefore, try not to be another Fool; but, Educate yourself before you even Test it: beCause, it is also Possible for you to Discourage yourself by Breaking the Rules, whereby you might Presume Things unto your own Destruction: beCause of your PRIDE. Yes, it Requires a Humble Honest Mind to Accomplish Great Things with God, who does not Want nor Need any Ignorant Fools in his Great Kingdom, which is a Good Government, which is Reserved for the RIGHTEOUS Ones, who are HOLY in Mind, Spirit and Body. Therefore, do not Presume that you Know anything for Sure, until it is Proven, at: "The GREAT Worldwide TELEVISED Court HEARING!" (That Great Meeting of the Most-Intelligent and Well-Educated Minds!) By The Worldwide People's Revolution!® Book 041B. ‡

— Chapter 08 —

Will any Intelligent Reader Skip Over Chapter 07?

08-01 |_| The short Answer is, NO — no Intelligent Readers will Skip Over Chapter 07; but, a few will Attempt to Skip Around it, after reading it: beCause it Contradicts their False Doctrines, which can easily be Proven to be False in a Courtroom, with Unholy Mutilated Bibles in Hands and Hearts. For Example, there is that Famous Christian Quotation from *Second Chronicles 7:14,* which should read something like this: *If my Chosen People, who are Called by my Name, will Humble themselves by Means of Fasting and Praying, until they become like Innocent Children with Clean Bodies and Purified Minds, and Pray for Forgiveness of all of their Sins, and Seek the Holiness of my Face in their own Faces, and Turn Away from all of their Wicked Ways, then I will Hear their Cry from Heaven, and will Forgive all of their Sins, and Cleanse them from all Unrighteousness, and will also Heal their Lands, whereby they will Produce an Abundance of Sweet Juicy Fruits, which are the Life of Mankind, which is WHY it is called the Tree of Life: beCause the Life is in the Blood, and the Blood is Constructed by the Life that is found in the Sweet Juicy Fruits, Green Leaves, Nuts, and Fresh Vegetables, which are Survival Foods, which can be Eaten when there are no Fruits on the Trees to Eat, nor any Dried Fruits in the Walk-in Cooler, nor any Dried Nuts in the Walk-in Freezer, which can and should have a hundred-year Supply of all such Fruits, Green Leaves, Nuts, and other Foods: beCause it is Wise to be Prepared for any Great Famines that might come: beCause Satan is Busy, making a Way to Destroy Souls, even as he did for the Children of Jobe. Therefore, do not be Fools like them; but, be Wise for yourselves, and Build Beautiful Planned City States in Great Stone Terraces, whereby all of your Gardens, Vineyards, and Orchards can be Planted and Cared for within those Terraces: beCause, your* "Beautiful Swanky Stone Dome Home COMPLEXES!" (HOW to Build SECURE Tax-proof, Insurance-proof, Self-air-conditioned, Paint-proof, Rot-proof, Termite-proof, Mouse-proof, Fireproof, Tornado-proof, Hurricane-proof, Thief-proof, and BOMB-PROOF Houses!) By The Worldwide People's Revolution!® Book 102, will be within those Great Stone Terraces, which will be True Homeland Security for Wise People, who will not have any Bills to Pay, if they Act Wisely, and Join: "The Swanky Associations of Working Soldiers!" (A Fascinating Collection of

Various Kinds of Voluntary Working Soldiers!) By The Worldwide People's Revolution!® Book 018B, who will Organize themselves Better than the Army Ants and Honey Bees, who will be Wise and Exercise their DUMBmocracy, and "VOTE for The GOAT!" (The New Political Party that has Guaranteed Solutions for our Massive Problems!) By The Worldwide People's Revolution!® Book 109: beCause you must Establish "The New RIGHTEOUS One-World Government!" (HOW to Establish a Righteous One-World Government without Going to WAR!) By The Worldwide People's Revolution!® Book 056, whose Headquarters should be within "The Great World TEMPLE of PEACE!" (The Glory of Jerusalem Arises Again in the Great State of Flexible Texas!) By The Worldwide People's Revolution!® Book 017B, which should be within "A New Jerusalem in the Great State of Flexible Texas!" (HOW to make Good Use of the Mississippi River!) By The Worldwide People's Revolution!® Book 090: beCause there is Plenty of Open Space there to Build it, which is also in a Central Location for North and Central America, which should be Designed to Contain no less than a Billion Wise People, who should also Build Greenhouses and Fruit Tree Houses for Tropical Fruits and Nuts: beCause it is Good to have a Great Variety of Foods to Eat, at those "Royal Swanky Buffets!" (The Best Feasts in the Whole World!) By The Worldwide People's Revolution!® Book 103: beCause, that is WHY that I Created all such Good Foods, for Good People to Richly Enjoy. However, that is not to say that you would make Fat Walruses of yourselves, just beCause of Lusting after more Foods than you Need to Eat; but, it is only to say that those Foods are Available to Eat in Moderation, unless you are Working Hard, in which Case you may Eat more, according to your Appetite. However, when you Discover that you are Lusting after Forbidden Flesh, it is Time to Do some Fasting and Praying, which the Children of Israel should have Done, rather than make Fools of themselves by Glutting themselves on Quails in Various Ways, who Fried it, Baked it, Boiled it, and Spiced it just Right, according to their Appetites, whereby thousands of them Died from it: beCause Flesh is not Exactly the Ideal Food to be Eating, if you Want to be Healthy, Wealthy, and Wise. ‡ (See: *Numbers 11, and Psalm 78.*)

08-02 [_] O Good Pastor of Uncommon Sense, those are not the Exact Words of *Second Chronicles 7:14,* and you Know it, and everyone else Knows it, including myself; but, I do Wish to God that all of those Good Words had been in our Unholy Mutilated Bibles, all along, whereby we might have been Inspired to Build those **"GLORIOUS Swanky Hotels Castles and Fortresses!" (Beautiful Planned City States for WISE Intelligent Well-Educated People with Common Sense and Good**

Understanding!) **By The Worldwide People's Revolution!®** Book 019B, with Millions of those "Beautiful Swanky PALACES!" (A New Concept in Living Habits — Swanky Palaces for Poor People!) By The Worldwide People's Revolution!® Book 066, whereby we could have Avoided all of those Endless Bills to Pay, and Countless Pills to Consume: beCause of Feasting on Sweet Juicy Fruits from the Trees of Life, which will be Satisfying to our Souls, if we just Eat them in Moderation, and do not Lust after them: beCause Lusts Overstimulate a Person's Appetite. Moreover, we must also have someone to LOVE: beCause, True Love makes it Possible to NOT Lust after any Forbidden Things. Therefore, no one should be Deprived of True Love, which is perhaps more Important than Eating Correctly: beCause Happiness Depends on a Satisfied Mind, which a Lonely Person cannot have. †§‡

08-03 [_] Well, my Friend, when you are Close to God, it is Difficult to be Lonely; but, I Agree that everyone Needs someone to Love, who Truly Loves them: beCause, Flesh-to-Flesh Contact is a Necessity for Good Mental Health, which is what is WRong with Prisons, and especially with Isolation in "Solitary Confinement," as the Criminals-in-Charge call it. In Fact, a lot of those Manufactured Criminals most likely became Criminals for a Lack of Attention, at Home: beCause of Parents being too Busy, Earning a Living, when they should have been Free to Attend to their Children, which they would be in the Swanky Fortress System. ‡

08-04 [_] O Good Pastor of Uncommon Sense, there are some Places in this World of Woes — such as Amsterdam, Holland — where the Cost of Living is beyond the Ability of Young People to Pay for it, who have to Liv in little Prison Camps, you might say, without any Gardens, at all, much less, those SPACIOUS "Beautiful Swanky Stone Dome Home COMPLEXES!" (HOW to Build SECURE Tax-proof, Insurance-proof, Self-air-conditioned, Paint-proof, Rot-proof, Termite-proof, Mouse-proof, Fireproof, Tornado-proof, Hurricane-proof, Thief-proof, and BOMB-PROOF Houses!) By The Worldwide People's Revolution!® Book 102. So, they would Think that they Died and went to Heaven, if they got to Liv in such Beautiful Places. {See: "Do People Go to Heaven when they Die?" (The Unbelievable Truth about Life and Death!) **By The Good Pastor of Uncommon Sense!** Book 120.}

08-05 [_] Well, my Friend, there are many YouTube Videos, which Reveal some of the Truths about Living Conditions, all around the World, and few Places are as Bad as Crowded Cities of Confusion, where Crimes are also much Higher than in the Countryside, Farmlands and

Wilderness Areas, which is to be Expected: beCause of the Intense Competition among Capitalists. However, Life on the Farm can also be very Bad, if there are many Bills to Pay: beCause most Farmers are Relying on Rains, which can Fail, which would not be the Case at Swanky Fortresses, which would have an Abundance of Water in their Cisterns, even if they had to Import it from the Amazon River, in the Atlantic Ocean, using Solar-powered Water Ships: beCause that is Practical.

08-06 [_] O Good Pastor of Uncommon Sense, I am Greatly Concerned about People Rejecting the Provable Truths in Chapter 07, whereby they could Condemn themselves: beCause of not even Attempting to REPENT: beCause of Sincerely Believing that they have been "Saved," and are going to Heaven when they Die, just beCause of having a Spiritual Experience with God, who was only Trying to Encourage them to Keep Pursuing that Line of Thinking, and Hopefully get them Converted from Sinners into Saints, which might Happen to one in 10,000 People or more, which is a very Sad Story: beCause it is Possible for ALL of the People to Repent, even as the Entire City of Nineveh Repented, and were Glad that they did. However, most Americans are Afraid of Fasting: beCause they Vainly Imagine that they might Die, if they just Missed Eating a Meal or 2.

08-07 [_] Well, my Friend, that is one of the Reasons that I call it the Hopeless Church of Little Faith: beCause they are not Willing to even Experiment with Fasting, in spite of it being a Good Time to Experiment: beCause of the Bug. Moreover, if a Person has a Job, he Feels that he cannot take a Chance on Losing that Job. Therefore, how is he supposed to Repent in a World like this?‡

08-08 [_] O Good Pastor of Uncommon Sense, do you not know that we Christians are Saved by GRACE, alone; and NOT by the Works of Fasting, nor Praying? In Fact, that was the Big Contention between the Catholic Church and the Protestors, called Protestants, who Argued that it was not Necessary for Sinners to Repent by Fasting, nor by Praying: beCause they were Saved by Grace, whereby they only had to say, "Oh Lordy, I Bleevz in yu, and thank you for Saving my Soul," whereby they Greatly Deceived themselves, and became Converts like the Grahamites, whom you call Graceful Sinners, who Suffer with all Kinds of Ailments: beCause of not Actually being Saved from all of their Sins, if any of them, who are most often Liars and Hypocrites! †§‡§§

08-09 [_] Well, my Friend, if it were that Easy to Obtain a Position in the Government of God, just by saying: "Oh Lord, I Believe in thee," almost everyone would have such a Position; but, Jesus said, *"Even though you draw near unto me, even into my Bosom; but, do not Keep my Commandments, I will Cast you Out, and say to you during the Day of Judgment: 'Depart from me, O you Workers of Iniquities: beCause I never Knew you': beCause True Love Requires Obedience."* — *NMV.* And again, he said, *"If you Love me, Keep my Commandments, and then I will Love you, and will come Visit you, and will Send the Holy Spirit to Comfort you."* — *John 14.*

08-10 [_] O Good Pastor of Uncommon Sense, I will take my Chances on being Saved by Grace, even if I am nothing but a Lying Hypocrite: beCause I Trust God to be Merciful to me, and Overlook my Disobedience to his Commandments. After all, Laws were made to be Broken. †§‡

— Chapter 09 —

What should the Hopeless Church of Little Faith Do to Save itself?

09-01 [_] Well, they should Repent of all of their Sins, and especially of their Dietary Sins: beCause those Sins Cause most of the other Sins, even though "The Root Cause for almost all Evils!" (The Strange Things that People Say and Do to Get more Money!) By The Worldwide People's Revolution!® Book 078, is "For the Love of Money!" (The Strange Things that People Say and Do to Get more Money!) By The Worldwide People's Revolution!® Book 003B. But, what is it that Inspires the Love of Money, if not to Consume all Kinds of Tasty Things that cannot be Found in the Wilderness of Temptations, which actually has no Temptations at all, unless Satan is there? Indeed, a Horse or Cow is Contented with some Grasses and Grains to Eat; but, People have all Kinds of LUSTS, once they Taste of Strange Foods, which they can hardly Resist Eating, if those Foods Taste Really Good to them. Strangely enough, most of the Forbidden Foods seem to Taste Good, once you get used to Eating them; but, not Really Good, like a Mango should. Therefore, Addicted Parents often Force their Babies to Eat those Forbidden Foods: beCause they are Normally Cheaper than Good Foods, which is Normal for Capitalism; but, it would not be the Case within Swanky Fortresses: beCause, their Main Goal would be to Produce Good Wholesome Natural Foods and Drinks, whereby they might be Healthy, Wealthy, and Wise.

09-02 [_] O Good Pastor of Uncommon Sense, those Forbidden Foods are Temptations of Satan, who Enjoys Destroying the Lives of Ignorant People, even as he has done with the Kuroonu Viirus. Therefore, he begins with Candies, Cookies, and other Sweet Things, which the Children Like: beCause they have a Natural Craving for Sweet Fruits, which is True for all Peoples, Worldwide.

09-03 [_] Well, my Friend, few Things in this World of Wonders are as Tricky and Deceiving as Forbidden Foods. For Example, Butchers put Sugar and Salt into Hams, before Smoking them with Apple Wood, or Hickory, which makes those Hams Taste Extremely Good to a Hungry Person, who can easily get Addicted to Eating them. Therefore, anyone can easily Understand the Garden of Eden Story about the Forbidden Fruit on the Tree that Represented the Nolij of All that is Good and Evil, which Mother Eve could not Resist: beCause the Temptation was too Great, whereby all of her Dawterz were also Deceived by Forbidden Foods, who are still being Deceived by them: beCause that is HOW Satan gets through the Doorways of our Hearts, through our Stomachs, you might say, even though it is Normally through our Eyeballs; or, if we are Blind, it is by our Taste Buds. But, one Way or another, once we Yield to the Great Temptation, and Eat something that is Forbidden, we are generally "Hooked," or Trapped by it, which is where Advertisements come in Handy for the Pit Diggers, who put up Road Signs, Tempting us to Try whatever can be Found in their Bottomless Pits, which are Spiced just Right — such as in the Barbecue Pits in the Deep South of "The Divided States of United Lies!" (The so-called "United States of North America" in Disguise!) By The Worldwide People's Revolution!® Book 058.

09-04 [_] O Good Pastor of Uncommon Sense, King Solomon Warned us, saying: *"He who Digs a Pit for other People to Fall into, shall Fall into his own Pit, or someone else's Pit; and he who Rolls a Stone down a Hill to Kill someone, shall have it Rolled Back at him."* — *Proverbs 26:27 and Ecclesiastes 10:8.* In other Words, we Reap whatever we Soo, which the Hindus call *Karma.*

09-05 [_] Well, my Friend, if Karma always Worked, like Gravity, a Person might Rely on it for getting Revenge; but, it seems that the God of Karma is most often Sleeping, nowadays: beCause the Most-Vile and Evil People seem to get by with their High Crimes in Low Places — such as on Wall Street, whereby Rich Bankers have Robbed People of their Houses, Farms, Businesses and other Properties, without any Retributions or Justices, even as our Selected King was Robbed of his 40-acre Farm in Arkansas, after Investing 300,000 dollars in it, plus 30 Years of Hard Labor. For Example, here is a Small Part of his 2,000-square-feet Rock Ceiling in his 98% Rock House.

09-06 [_] Yes, there is a Small Part of his Algerian Onyx Floors, which are Worth far more than any Ugly Stinking Carpets: beCause each Onyx Tile is Unique and Special, while Carpets are not at all Special. Indeed, it was God who Created the Onyx, while Capitalists Invented the Carpets. ‡

09-07 [_] O Good Pastor of Uncommon Sense, that Sad Story can be found in: "LIGHTNING STRIKES Versus Lightning Bugs!" (HOW you can Become Moderately RICH, without Telling any Lies nor

97

Selling any Trash!) By The Worldwide People's Revolution!® Book 074.

09-08 [_] Well, my Friend, not only can anyone Find that Sad Story; but, they can also Find the Best Solution for Solving all such Problems, if they just take the Time to Read that Inspired Book.

09-09 [_] O Good Pastor of Uncommon Sense, getting Ignorant People to Read Books with Honest Open Minds, is more Difficult than Pulling Out Horses' Teeths with Tweezers. In Fact, it is almost Impossible, once they get their Heads Stuck in one or the other of those 2 Stinking Holes in: "The BIG White OUTHOUSE on the Not-so-Biblical Capitol DUNGHILL!" (The Chief Sins of the Divided States of United Lies!) By The Worldwide People's Revolution!® Book 023B. †§

09-10 [_] Well, my Friend, when they do not find that Statement to be very Funny, they have Lost their Sense of Humor, which is Proof that they Belong to "The Hopeless Church of Little Faith!" (The Unholy Church of Graceful Sinners, who are Mostly just Liars and Hypocrites!) **By** The Good Pastor of Uncommon Sense! Book 121. Otherwise, they would be Shouting for JOY, just to Read: "Our Selected King SPEAKS OUT!" (It is High Time for some Sane Person to get Total Control of this Insane World!) By The Worldwide People's Revolution!® Book 100!

— Chapter 10 —

The Conclusion

10-01 [_] Most Professing "Christians" will Confess that it is Bad to Drive those Polluting Vehicles on Endless Highways — not only beCause of the Pollution and Horrible Expenses of it; and not only beCause of the Millions of People who DIE from it; but, also beCause God HATES it: beCause he Hates ALL that is EVIL, and Loves All that is GOOD; and there is nothing Good about those Bloody Gory Accidents, much less, those Gory Hateful WARS, which only Profit the Lying Conniving Edomites, including the Car Manufacturers, who also make War Machines. Meanwhile, the Tax Slaves Bear the Financial Burdens of it, who would Like to be Liberated; but, they do not Know HOW. Moreover, neither the Snooze Reporters, Preachers, Teachers, Professors, Scientists, Doctors, Lawyers, Judges, nor Politicians ever Mention those **"GLORIOUS Swanky Hotels Castles and Fortresses!" (Beautiful Planned City States for WISE Intelligent Well-Educated People with Common Sense and Good Understanding!) By The Worldwide People's Revolution!®** Book 019B, in spite of their Great Advantages over these Cities of Confusion. †§‡

10-02 [_] So, O Good Pastor of Uncommon Sense, would you Tear Down New York City, for Example, just to Build a Swanky Fortress over there?

10-03 [_] Well, my Friend, most of New Yuck City is just a Trash Dump, with Billions of Rats running about in Old Ugly Stinking Highrise Apartments, without Working Elevators, whereby the Old People have to Climb Up Stairways, just to get to their Rat-infested Apartments, which would all come Down during a Severe Earthquake: beCause they do not have Reinforced Concrete, nor Steel to hold them Together. They are a Disaster waiting to Happen. Nevertheless, our Selected King does not Object to leaving them stand there, if Ignorant People Want to Liv within them; but, for all of the Sane People, there should be a Way for them to Escape, and to Raise their Standard of Living by at least 100 Times! Therefore, we should Immediately begin to Build Swanky Fortresses, all around the World, for whomever Sincerely Wants to Prosper in a Righteous Way.‡

10-04 [_] O Good Pastor of Uncommon Sense, most Professing "Christians" Plan on going to Heaven when they Die. Therefore, they are not Interested in Helping to Build any "GLORIOUS Swanky Hotels Castles and Fortresses!" (Beautiful Planned City States for WISE Intelligent Well-Educated People with Common Sense and Good Understanding!) By The Worldwide People's Revolution!® Book 019B. Moreover, without their Help, none will ever get Built: beCause Sinners cannot be Trusted to Do any Good Works like that. Only Reliable True Christians can be Fully Trusted; and, as far as I know, they all Died and went to Heaven, Centuries Ago! †§‡

10-05 [_] Well, my Friend, if there are no Honest Hardworking People left Alive on this Good Earth, we are in BIG Trouble: beCause that is what is Required to Accomplish any such Great Things. Therefore, if you are Correct, it is Truly the Hopeless Church of Little Faith! Therefore, I would say that they Deserve to DIE for their Rebellion; and therefore, I Pray that they will be Cursed with the 7 Last Great Plagues, if they Reject the Great Truths that I Teach. {See: "Do People Go to Heaven when they Die?" (The Unbelievable Truth about Life and Death!) By The Good Pastor of Uncommon Sense! Book 120.}

10-06 [_] O Good Pastor of Uncommon Sense, why is it that People like to Suffer so much? One would Think that they would be very Happy to Hear about those "GLORIOUS Swanky Hotels Castles and Fortresses!" (Beautiful Planned City States for WISE Intelligent Well-Educated People with Common Sense and Good Understanding!) By The Worldwide People's Revolution!® Book 019B, and have Hope for Moving into them, just to Solve their Massive Problems. For Example, there are no Icy Slippery Streets: beCause of using Underground Tunnels with Electric Elevators, Escalators, and Quiet Pollution-free Subway Trains, which run on Smooth Railroad Tracks, which are 12 feet Wide: beCause the Spacious Railcars are 20 feet Wide, 100 feet Long, and 12 feet High, and Designed to Carry Quadracycles, Bicycles, and Millions of Passengers, if they are Needed, while being Entertained with the Latest Good News Reports on large TV Screens. They also have Comfortable Recliners to Rest in, if they are Slow Trains. Even the Fast Trains have Comfortable Padded Seats to Rest on. Moreover, all of the Trains are on Time, never Late, never in a Traffic Jam, never in any Accidents, and never Overcrowded, which also have Conductors to Help the Passengers to Find the Correct Stops and Train Stations for all Points of Interest, including other Swanky Fortresses. Indeed, each Train runs on its own Private Tracks, and only in one Direction around the Fortress. So, if you want to go in the other Direction, you have to take an Elevator to the next Terrace, to get on a Train that runs in that Direction. The Conductors will be Happy to Send you with a Personal Escort, if you Ask for Help: beCause, **"The Swanky Association of Convenient Transportation,"** has lots of Volunteers to do that Work. ‡

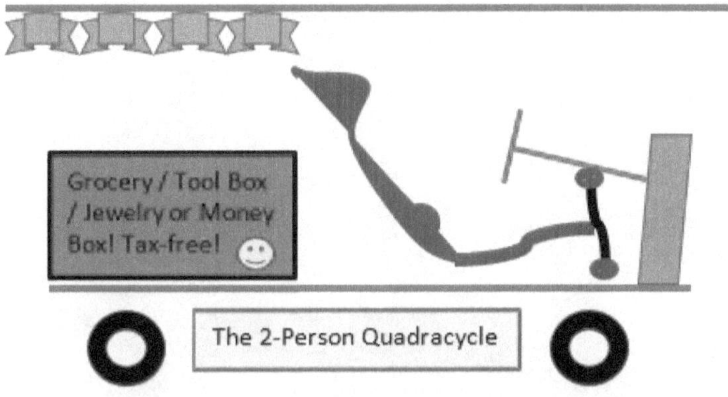

10-07 [_] So, my Friend, if a Person Wanted to go Visit his Aunt Polly, or the Widow Douglas, he could Load his Gifts and Suitcases onto his Quadracycle, and Drive it into a Spacious Elevator, and from there into one of those Spacious Railcars, and take a Ride to another Swanky Fortress, and Set his Telephone to Wake him Up just before Arriving there, at the Exact Exit: beCause of getting a Free Smart Phone at one of those Swanky Tool Houses, which could also make a Custom-made Quadracycle, whereby everything Fits Perfectly, which could also have a Hand-carved Leather Seat to sit on, or whatever that Person Likes: beCause each Member of **"The Swanky Associations of Working Soldiers!" (A Fascinating Collection of Various Kinds of Voluntary Working Soldiers!) By The Worldwide People's Revolution!® Book 018B**, would be Well-Trained to Do his or her Job, rather than Waste a lot of Precious Time in: **"The Public School of IGNERUNT FQLZ!" (HOW we have been GRAATLEE DISEEVD by Capitalism!) By The Worldwide People's Revolution!®** Book 024B. In Fact, if a Student Proved to be Talented, he or she could Select whatever Occupation that he or she Likes Best, and Volunteer for it, and get Well-Trained to Do Professional Work, whereby he or she could Train other Students to Do the same, as a Private School Teacher, even if he or she is only a Teenager. For Example, let us say that some 12-year-old Boy wants to become a Leather Carver: beCause of Seeing this Picture —

10-08 [_] Therefore, he would Join **"The Swanky Association of Professional Leather Carvers,"** who would Train him Correctly at the Swanky Castle, whereby he could Train other Students Correctly, whose Work would be Inspected by the Master Leather Carver, who would Grade him, and Award him with a Certificate for being a Professional Leather Carver, who might become a Professional Teacher for that Good Work, and eventually become a Master Leather Carver, himself: beCause it Requires Years of Careful Work to become such a Master; but, once he has Succeeded at it, he would become Eligible to Liv in one of those Special "Beautiful Swanky PALACES!" (A New Concept in

Living Habits — Swanky Palaces for Poor People!) By The Worldwide People's Revolution!® Book 066, just for Professional Leather Carvers! Moreover, each Swanky Fortress would have such Palaces, if they Wanted them. Some would Naturally NOT Want them: beCause of being Strict VEGANS, who would Object to Eating Meats, and making anything with Leather: beCause they would Prefer to use Cloth, Hemp, Glass, Wood, or some other Natural Materials. Indeed, each Person will Fill Out and File: **"The Complete SURVEYS of our VALUES!" (SURVEYS of Religious Spiritual Political Governmental Sexual Social Moral Economical Business Labor Habitual and Miscellaneous VALUES!) By The Worldwide People's Revolution!®** Book 059, whereby they can easily Discover other People of Like-mindedness, whereby they can all Liv in PEACE, and be HAPPY with their God!‡

10-09 [_] For Example, some People will Object to Using any of the hundreds of thousands of Mountains of Rocks in this World of Wonders; but, they will not Object to making Ceramic Tiles with Solar Power and Electric Kilns for Baking the Tiles. Therefore, they will come up with Fantastic Hotels, Castles and Fortresses, like the People of the World have never Seen before. After all, there are Billions of People with Unlimited Imaginations, who can now Set their Minds on GOOD Things, and Forget about going to War, and also Forget about Paying Taxes to Satan.‡

10-10 [_] O Good Pastor of Uncommon Sense, are you saying that if we Want to become Body Builders, that we will have Free Gymnasiums and all of the Various Kinds of Exercise Machines to Play with? Will we also get to Wrestle Naked with whomever we Love, and Enjoy the Bodies of

Beautiful Young Men with Silky Skins? Will that be Permissible at all Swanky Fortresses? †§‡

10-11 [_] Well, my Friend, there will be all Kinds of Swanky Hotels, Castles and Fortresses. Therefore, you only have to Check the Correct Boxes in "The Complete SURVEYS of our VALUES!" (SURVEYS of Religious Spiritual Political Governmental Sexual Social Moral Economical Business Labor Habitual and Miscellaneous VALUES!) By The Worldwide People's Revolution!® Book 059, and you can get to Liv with Like-minded People, including those Body Builders, who may only come to Visit your Swanky Castle on Special Occasions: beCause of having other Ambitions, which may be Fulfilled in other Swanky Fortresses. Therefore, you will only have to Search for whatever you Want on the Internet, and you will Find it, once we get everything Set Up Properly, which will Require a few Years, and less Years, if we get to Work on it, right NOW! Therefore, you should Inform all of your Friends and Naaberz about it: beCause it is Possible to "VOTE for The GOAT!" (The New Political Party that has Guaranteed Solutions for our Massive Problems!) By The Worldwide People's Revolution!® Book 109. Indeed, you should read: "The CONDENSED Version of MARK TWAIN Races for the PRESIDENCY with a Landslide VICTORY!" (The 2020 Presidential Candidates Desperately Need Some STRONG Undefeatable COMPETITION!) By The Worldwide People's Revolution!® Book 033C, which is a very Enlightening Book with Great Inspiration. ‡

10-12 [_] O Good Pastor of Uncommon Sense, suppose that I Want to Wrestle Naked with the Pretty Girls with Big Breasts at Swanky Castles — will that be Permissible in any Fortresses? †§‡

10-13 [_] Well, it might be Permissible at certain Swanky Castles; but, I Suggest that you get Married, and then you can Wrestle with your Naked Wife every Night, if she Wants to, and with a Good Conscience; but, be Aware that a Baby might come along and Upset your Plans for a while. After all, Things like that Happen, nowadays; but, if you Want to Avoid it, I Suggest that you be Wise and Wrestle with the Men, only: beCause they cannot get Pregnant, nor get you Pregnant. †§‡

10-14 [_] O Good Pastor of Uncommon Sense, I Prefer to Find someone who Loves me, and be Contented with FIDELITY, which God Loves Most. Therefore, HOW will I Discover that Like-minded Person in a Perverse World like this?

10-15 [_] Well, my Friend, the Computers can Discover that Person for you, if the Correct Information is Fed into those Computers, which is WHY that everyone should Fill Out and File: "The Complete SURVEYS of our VALUES!" (SURVEYS of Religious Spiritual Political Governmental Sexual Social Moral Economical Business Labor Habitual and Miscellaneous VALUES!) By The Worldwide

People's Revolution!® Book 059, and not be Worried about any Beastly Wicked Government using that Information against you, if I am in Charge of Things: beCause, I Believe that everyone should have the Freedom to Say and Do whatever they Like; but, only with other People of Like-mindedness: beCause it is not Right to Contaminate Innocent Minds with Perverse Sex Stories — such as one can Discover in: "The New MAGNIFIED Version of the Book of ACTS!" (The Understandable Version of the Acts of the Apostles in Plain English!) By The Worldwide People's Revolution!® Book 063, which tells about the Apostle Paul and his Beloved Timothy, whom he Circumcised. Indeed, you Honestly never Heard anything quite like it during your entire Life! I Mean it — it is one Really Fantastic Sexy Biblical Story, which I Highly Recommend for the Hopeless Church of Little Faith, which Doubts it! †§‡§§

— Chapter 40 —

A Long List of other Fascinating Literature by the same Inspired Author

[_] 40-001 — "LIGHTNING Versus the Lightning Bug!" (HOW almost Everyone can become Moderately RICH, without Telling Any Lies nor Selling Any Capitalist Trash!) By The Worldwide People's Revolution!® Book 001B.

[_] 40-002 — "What is WRong with those Professing Christians?" (A Self-Examination of the Heart of the Body of Good Government!) By The Worldwide People's Revolution!® Book 002B.

[_] 40-003 — "For the Love of Money!" (The Strange Things that People Say and Do to Get more Money!) By The Worldwide People's Revolution!® Book 003B.

[_] 40-004 — "How Best to Prepare for CLIMATE CHANGES!" (The Wisest Plan for Mankind to Follow!) By The Worldwide People's Revolution!® Book 004B.

[_] 40-005 — "Why do I have to be Surrounded by CRAZY PEOPLE!" (Do almost all People Feel like they are Surrounded by CRAZY People?) By The Worldwide People's Revolution!® Book 005B.

[_] 40-006 — "The Washington Journal is a FARCE! (C-SPAN Managers are not very WISE!) By The Worldwide People's Revolution!® Book 006C. (This Book has lots of Good Humor.)

[_] 40-007 — "The PRAYERS of PUMPKINHEADS!" (This Book is otherwise known as the Prayers of Preachers, Priests, Professors, Politicians, Prostitutes, Policemen, Pumpkinheads, Punks, Prisoners, and other Professionals — in other Words, the Capital P People!) By The Worldwide People's Revolution!® Book 007B. (Some of it is for Adults only.)

[_] 40-008 — "A Sound Argument for Good Masters and Obedient Servants!" (WHY Everyone Needs a Good Master, and every

Master Needs Good Obedient Servants!) By The Worldwide People's Revolution!® Book 008B.

[_] 40-009 — "WHY are some Preachers so POOR?" (HOW almost all Preachers can Get Moderately RICH, without Preaching any Outlandish LIES!) By The Worldwide People's Revolution!® Book 009B.

[_] 40-010 — "GOOD NEWS for REBEL WOMEN!" (HOW almost all Wives can become Moderately RICH without Leaving their Homes! Guaranteed!) By The Worldwide People's Revolution!® Book 010B.

[_] 40-011 — "The Low Court of Supreme Injustices is Brought to Trial!" (Our Selected King Butts Heads with the United States Supreme Court, with or without their Black Robes of Hypocrisies and Lies!) By The Worldwide People's Revolution!® Book 011B. (This Inspired Book contains the Famous *Declaration of Interdependence,* which is a Must Read. It also contains the Correct Wording for the Placard on the Statue of Liberty.)

[_] 40-012 — "The Right Design for Living!" (A List of Great Advantages for Building Beautiful Planned City States!) By The Worldwide People's Revolution!® Book 012B. (This Book contains many Important Drawings, as well as HOW to Save hundreds of Trillions of Dollars by Building Swanky Fortresses, and Living in Peace within them. It is a Companion Book of Book 011B, which contains many more Great Advantages for Swanky Fortresses.)

[_] 40-013 — **"The Gospel According to The Worldwide People's Revolution!®" (The Good News from the Most Modern Perspective!)** See Book 077. (This Book contains the Famous Sermon of Jonah to the Ninevites, whereby 120,000 People Repented in Sackcloth and Ashes! Do not Miss Out on it. Not even the Rev. Dr. Billy Graham got 120,000 Converts during one Day!)

[_] 40-014 — **"Poverty Hunger Riots Strikes Police Brutalities Election Deceptions and Civil Wars!" (The High Price that we Earthlings have Paid for Leaving the Good Land!) By The Worldwide People's Revolution!® Book 014B.**

[_] 40-015 — **"Seven Great Armies of Working Soldiers!" (HOW to Provide a Way for Everyone to WORK: so as to Eliminate Poverty,**

Crimes, Drug Abuses, Prisons and Unnecessary Taxes!) By The Worldwide People's Revolution!® Book 015B. (This Book contains a True-Life Story when the Author was in the Army.)

[_] 40-016 — "The CONSTITUTION for the New RIGHTEOUS One-World Government!" (HOW all Peoples can get True Justice, and Celebrate the Great Year of JUBILEE!) By The Worldwide People's Revolution!® Book 016B.

[_] 40-017 — "The Great World TEMPLE of PEACE!" (The Glory of Jerusalem Arises Again in the Great State of Flexible Texas!) By The Worldwide People's Revolution!® Book 017B.

[_] 40-018 — "The Swanky Associations of Working Soldiers!" (A Fascinating Collection of Various Kinds of Voluntary Working Soldiers!) By The Worldwide People's Revolution!® Book 018B. (There will be thousands of Associations for all Kinds of Occupations, which will Specialize in Fine Arts — such as Hand-carved Leather-bound Books. See "LIGHTNING STRIKES Versus Lightning Bugs!" (HOW you can Become Moderately RICH, without Telling any Lies nor Selling any Trash!) By The Worldwide People's Revolution!® Book 074, for a Picture of a Good Example.)

[_] 40-019 — "GLORIOUS Swanky Hotels Castles and Fortresses!" (Beautiful Planned City States for WISE Intelligent Well-Educated People with Common Sense and Good Understanding!) By The Worldwide People's Revolution!® Book 019B. (This Book contains many Rough Drawings, which could be Greatly Improved upon by someone who Knows the Art, and has the Correct Computer Programs for doing it.)

[_] 40-020 — "Are you a Jobless Graduate of the SKQL uv FQLZ?" (HOW to Get a GOUD EJUKAASHUN without Robbing the Bank!) By The Worldwide People's Revolution!® Book 020B. (This Inspired Book contains the New MAGNIFIED Version {NMV} of *First Corinthians 13*, plus: HOW to Produce Pure Living Water!)

[_] 40-021 — "The LUSCIOUS All-Mineral Organic Method of Gardening!" (HOW to Grow DELICIOUS Satisfying Foods for Potential Kingz and Kweenz in Beautiful Swanky PALACES!) By The Worldwide People's Revolution!® Book 021B. (This Book Explains HOW to make a Flood-proof Garden, while Trapping the Rainwater.)

[_] 40-022 — **"Did God or Satan Ordain Medical Doctors?"** (Ask **Huck Finn and/or Nigger Jim: because neither Tom Sawyer nor Judge Thatcher would Know!**) **By The Worldwide People's Revolution!® Book 022B.** (This Inspired Book Reveals HOW to Prevent Common Colds, and has a Special Chapter that Explains what a True "Nigger" IS. Surprise yourself!)

[_] 40-023 — **"The BIG White OUTHOUSE on the Not-so-Biblical Capitol DUNGHILL!"** (**The Chief Sins of the Divided States of United Lies!**) **By The Worldwide People's Revolution!® Book 023B.** (This Book contains Special Words that most People have never Heard! Surprise yourself again!)

[_] 40-024 — **"The Public School of IGNERUNT FQLZ!"** (**HOW we have been GRAATLEE DISEEVD by Capitalism!**) **By The Worldwide People's Revolution!® Book 024B.** (This Book Teaches Children HOW to "Reed and Riit in Funetik Ingglish in just wun Daa!" You should Challenge your Frendz and Naaberz with it.)

[_] 40-025 — **"In thu Beeginingz uv Thingz!"** (**Thu Kreeaashun Stooree frum thu Beegining!**) **By The Worldwide People's Revolution!® Book 025B.** {The Original Cover Photo showed a Picture of a Golden Supootaa (Sapote), which not one Person in a Million has ever Tasted: because it does not Ship very well, in spite of it being one of the most Sweetest Pleasant Fruits known to Mankind, which must Ripen on the Tree to be Extremely Good, after it is Grown Properly by **"The LUSCIOUS All-Mineral Organic Method of Gardening!"** Book 021B, which Means that the Topsoil must have all of the Proper Minerals in it. Remember the Grapes of Eschol, which the Children of Israel brought back from the Promised Land in the *Book of Joshua,* which Required 2 Strong Men to Carry just one Cluster! See the Fascinating Photos in: **"Orgimmick Gardening at its Best!"** (**HOW to Grow Delicious Satisfying Foods without a 10 Million-Dollar Investment!**) **By The Worldwide People's Revolution!® Book 079.**}

[_] 40-026 — **"God Speaks and the Whole World Listens!"** (**Fire on the Mountain from the Burning Bush by the Spirit of Truths!**) **By The Worldwide People's Revolution!® Book 026B.** (This Powerful Book contains the Best Noah Story of all of the Books, including that of Gilgamesh the Great of Ancient Babylon!)

[_] 40-027 — **"Does a Good Soldier have to be a MURDERER?"** (**Seven Great Swanky Armies of Voluntary Working Soldiers!**) **By**

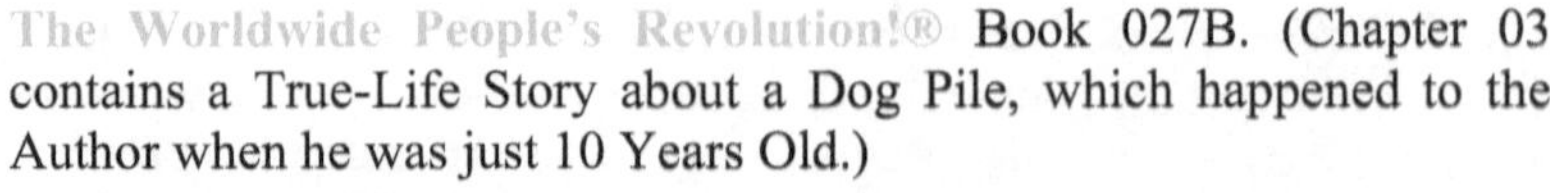

The Worldwide People's Revolution!® Book 027B. (Chapter 03 contains a True-Life Story about a Dog Pile, which happened to the Author when he was just 10 Years Old.)

[_] 40-028 — "Thu Nq MAGNUFIID Verzhun uv Thu PROVERBZ uv KING SOLUMUN in Plaan Ingglish!" (The Understandable Version of the Famous Proverbs of King Solomon in Plain English!) By The Worldwide People's Revolution!® Book 028. (This Marvelous Book MAGNIFIES each Proverb unto the Glory of the Great God of Inspiration, which is taken from the Original 4,000-page Book, which was written in less than 2 Months by the GIFT of Inspiration, which also contains the Famous Proverbs of Queen Izubelu!)

[_] 40-029 — "Unlimited Enerjee 99 Percent Pollutions Free!" (HOW to Obtain FREE ElecTrickery, Worldwide!) By The Worldwide People's Revolution!® Book 029. (This Book contains the Jackson Brower Suicide, among many other Fascinating Subjects.) The Updated Version is called: "UNLIMITED ENERGY 99 Percent Pollution-Free!" (HOW to Obtain Free ElecTrickery, Worldwide!) By The Worldwide People's Revolution!® Book 029B.

[_] 40-030 — "FREEDUM uv SPEECH!" (U Speshoul Maguzeen uv Onist Upinyunz!) By The Worldwide People's Revolution!® Book 030-0001, which contains the Great Advantages for Using Swanky Mulching Rocks in an All-Mineral Organic Garden, plus Baptism by Fire and Speaking in Foreign Languages! It is a Must Read. The Cover Photo shows a Portion of the Author's Marbleous Indian Countertop or Food Bar, which is just one Example of what you can also have in your own "Beautiful Swanky PALACES!" if you have the Honesty, Faith, Hope, Trust, Love, Patience, Persistence, Cooperation and OBEDIENCE that are Required for True Prosperity: beCause those are "The Seven Basic Spiritual Building Blocks of LIFE!" (Faith Hope Trust Love Patience Persistence and Obedience!) By The Worldwide People's Revolution!® Book 036! Therefore, Ejukaat yourself, and you will be Glad that you did!

[_] 40-031 — "A Sure Cure for GUN VIOLENCE!" (HOW TO STOP GANG WARS and CRIMINAL SHOOTINGS!) By The Worldwide People's Revolution!® Book 031. {The Cover Photo shows a Picture of a Short Shotgun, which is Fully Loaded with Double 00 Shells, and is Ready for any Tax Master who might Attempt to Steal the Retirement Home, who never moved a Finger to Help Build the Rock Houses, whereby we moved more than 66,666,666 Pounds by Hand, whose Property was Cunningly Stolen by that False Anti-Christ WICKED Cover-up Government, which allowed Bankers to Rob us of 30 Years of Hard Labor and more than 300,000 dollars-worth of Investments in our Uncommon American Farm, which is Explained in: "LIGHTNING STRIKES Versus Lightning Bugs!" (HOW you can Become Moderately RICH, without Telling any Lies nor Selling any Trash!) By The Worldwide People's Revolution!® Book 074, which contains many Photographs with Profound Explanations! Do not be left out in the Darkness of Ignorance. Get Informed, now: beCause, **"The Great False Economy is now DEBUNKED!"** Book 053.}

[_] 40-032 — "AIIRMWVC and Reasonable Solutions!" (Aliens, Illegal Immigrants, Refugees, Migrant Workers and other Victims of Capitalism!) By The Worldwide People's Revolution!® Book 032. (This Inspired Book contains *the New MAGNIFIED Version of Job 33.*)

[_] 40-033 — "MARK TWAIN Races for the PRESIDENCY with a Landslide VICTORY!" (The 2020 Presidential Candidates Desperately Need Some STRONG Undefeatable COMPETITION!) By The Worldwide People's Revolution!® Book 033B. {This Book contains a Part of the Author's Autobiography, and his Personal Answers to the Questions in: "The Complete SURVEYS of our VALUES!" (SURVEYS of Religious Spiritual Political Governmental Sexual Social Moral Economic Business Labor Habitual and Miscellaneous VALUES!) Book 059. **The CONDENSED Version** is Book 033C, which most People Prefer.}

[_] 40-034 — "ECCLESIASTES Uncovered and Recovered!" (The New MAGNIFIED Version of Ecclesiastes and the Song of Solomon in Plain English!) By The Worldwide People's Revolution!® Book 034. (This is the Book that contains the Famous Sayings for *"There is a Time to be Born, and a Time to Die ..."* which has been Greatly Magnified!)

[_] 40-035 — "The Environmentalists' Perfect Paradise!" (HOW almost Everyone can be Living in a Beautiful Manmade Paradise!) By The Worldwide People's Revolution!® Book 035C. (This Book contains the NMV of *Psalm 48,* which will Amaze you, O Lady Doubtfulness!)

[_] 40-036 — "The Seven Basic Spiritual Building Blocks of LIFE!" (Faith Hope Trust Love Patience Persistence and Obedience!) By The Worldwide People's Revolution!® Book 036. (This Book contains the Mockingbird's Version of *Hebrews 11,* plus the NMV of *First Corinthians 13,* among many other "Goodies.")

[_] 40-037 — "DIETS!" (A Reasonable Solution for the "Eternal Controversy"!) By The Worldwide People's Revolution!® Book 037.

[_] 40-038 — "The Nature of CAPITALISM!" (A List of the EVILS of CAPITALISM!) By The Worldwide People's Revolution!® Book 038.

[_] 40-039 — "SWANGKEENOMIKS Rules the Roost!" (HOW all People can Prosper in a RIIT WAA, and STOP Polluting the Earth with Capitalist TRASH!) By The Worldwide People's Revolution!® Book 039. (The Cover Photo shows a Portion of the Author's Retirement Home, before the 5,000+ square-feet Concrete Roof was Installed, after moving more than 66 Million Pounds by Hand, and mostly by his own Boastful Hands!)

[_] 40-040 — "The New MAGNIFIED Version of The Book of MORMON!" (The Story of the White and Dark Indians in the Americas!) By Big Chief Standsover Bull in River of Life! Book 040, which comes in 2 Volumes of about 500 Pages, each. The Cover Photo on the First Volume shows the Queen of England's Golden Coach, and the Cover Photo on the Second Volume shows one of many Polished Spanish Marble Walls in our Selected King's Retirement Home, which is worth a thousand dollars per square yard, which is another Example of what you can also have, if you simply OBEY your Righteous KING! All such Marble is very Inspiring. No one could Study it for very long without Believing in a Great Creator God. The Picture does not do it Justice. You would have to See it in Person, and Wash it with Pure Water to bring Out the Beauty of it.

[_] 40-041 — "The GREAT Worldwide TELEVISED Court HEARING!" (That Great Meeting of the Most-Intelligent and Well-Educated Minds!) By The Worldwide People's Revolution!® Book 041B. {This is the Book that the World has long been Waiting for: beCause it will Overthrow the Evil Empires, and make it Possible to Establish "The New RIGHTEOUS One-World Government!" (HOW to Establish a Righteous One-World Government without Going to WAR!) By The Worldwide People's Revolution!® Book 056. This is the Greatest Idea since the Invention of the Light Bulb, Guaranteed!}

[_] 40-042 — "The Secret City of the Great King!" (HOW the True Church will Escape from the Great Tribulation!) By The Worldwide People's Revolution!® Book 042. (Be Sure to Inform your Friends, Relatives and Naaberz about this Wonderful Book: beCause they might also Want to Escape!)

[_] 40-043 — "Terrorists Beware that your Days are Numbered!" (HOW to Bring those Terrorist Attacks to a Screeching HALT!) By The Worldwide People's Revolution!® Book 043. (This Book also contains the Fascinating Book of LEHI, which has now been Restored!) †‡

[_] 40-044 — "The New MAGNIFIED Version of ISAIAH in Plain English!" (The Understandable Version of the Book of Isaiah!) By The Worldwide People's Revolution!® Book 044. (The Cover Photo shows a Swanky Potato and Avocado Salad with Sweet Peas and Corn, among other "Secret" Ingredients, which are Revealed within the Book. Remember that you can read many Words for Free in the Book Previews on www.Amazon.com.usa or UK.)

[_] 40-045 — "HOW to Become a HOLY Man!" (40 Good Reasons WHY People Should FAST and PRAY!) By The Worldwide People's Revolution!® Book 045, which is a Companion Book of:

[_] 40-046 — "The Proper RULES for FASTING!" (The Complete Instruction Manual for True Repentance!) By The Worldwide People's Revolution!® Book 046, which is a Companion Book of the above-mentioned Book, which contains a True-Life Story about an Old Black Mare called Lucy, who Fasted for 30 Days without Food nor Water, who was Physiologically "Born Again," as Jesus might say. See the Full Details in: "The New MAGNIFIED Version of The GOOD NEWS According to Saint JOHN!" (The Gospel According to Saint John Zebedee Boanerges in Plain English!) Book 062, which contains many Inspiring Photographs with Explanations!

[_] 40-047 — "Are Americans the Most-STUPID People who ever Lived?" (HOW Working People can PROSPER and Live in PEACE Under the Rulership of a RIGHTEOUS KING!) By The Worldwide People's Revolution!® Book 047. (The Cover Photo shows a large Portion of the Author's Living Room Floor, which is worth 100,000$, which is just another Good Example of what you can also have, just for Loving and Obeying your Elected King!)

[_] 40-048 — "An Amazing Collection of Wit and Wisdom!" (The Marvelous Tale of the Colorful Peacock from Angel Ridge, and the Strong Rope of Everlasting Hope!) By The Worldwide People's Revolution!® Book 048. (The Cover Photo shows a Book Display, which will be Greatly Enhanced during the Future, when all 364+ Inspired Books are on Display in a Swanky Truth-brary, as Opposed to the Public LIE-brary.)

[_] 40-049 — "Justifications for Capitalizations!" (WHY our Selected King DEFIES the School of FOOLS by Capitalizing LOVE and HATE!) By The Worldwide People's Revolution!® Book 049.

[_] 40-050 — "The END of CONFUSION!" (The Great CELEBRATION of the Magnificent Wedding of the Most-Humble, Honest Nations, and the Grand Year of JUBILEE!) By The Worldwide People's Revolution!® Book 050. (Just Try to Visualize those **"Seven Great Swanky Armies of Voluntary Working Soldiers"** Marching through the Valley of Megiddo, being Dressed in their Colorful Robes, while the Band Plays *The Battle Hymn of the Republic,* and the Choirs Sing the Praises of the Great KING of Kings! What a Sight and Sound that will be, which will be Climaxed in "The Great World TEMPLE of PEACE," when the Nations will get Married, along with our Elected King! Come one, come all to "The GREAT Worldwide TELEVISED Court HEARING," by Means of your Wide Flat-screen TVs, whereby you might Learn WHY, WHEN and HOW!) †‡

[_] 40-051 — "The Loathsome Burdens of the Independent Jackasses!" (A New Civilized Approach for Quietly Solving our Massive Problems!) By The Worldwide People's Revolution!® Book 051. (Just Think about the Multitude of almost Worthless Meetings of the Minds, who Strained themselves to Think of Reasonable Solutions for our Massive Problems, who sometimes even Prayed to God for Help; but, the Best Solutions have been here for no less than 40 Years — Thanks to the Spirit of Inspiration from GOD!)

[_] 40-052 — "Are we Tax Slaves of a Lower Order than those Lying Conniving EDOMITES!" (HOW to be Liberated From all Forms of Slavery, Worldwide!) By The Worldwide People's Revolution!® Book 052B. {This Inspired Book once had another Title and Author, which was not Acceptable by Amazon, which has now been Restored in all of its Glory, and is Published by more Trustworthy People, who are not Afraid of Controversies, nor of: "The Swanky Sword of Divine

Truths!" (The Most-Powerful Weapon in the Whole Universe!) By The Worldwide People's Revolution!® Book 067.}

[_] 40-053 — "The Great False Economy is now DEBUNKED!" (Adolf Hitler had a much Better Economic System!) By The Worldwide People's Revolution!® Book 053. {Trust me, Adolf was no Saint; but, during the Day of God's Judgment, he will be Justified, while his Anti-Christ Opponents will be Condemned: beCause they Refused to Attend a Worldwide Radio Debate with Adolf Hitler, whose Arguments will Stand Up during the Day of Judgment, which would have Prevented World War 2, and thus Saved the Lives of no less than 60 Million People! Likewise, we Tax Slaves must now Act more Wisely, and DEMAND "The GREAT Worldwide TELEVISED Court HEARING," Book 041B, whereby we might Save the World from that Dreadful Battle of Megiddo, called *Armageddon!* Yes, the Ball is now in YOUR Hands, O Potential Friend or Enemy, and you are now Responsible for it. Therefore, do not Shirk your Duty as a Free Citizen; but, Help us to Spread this Message, far and wide, whereby the Masses of People will be Demanding The GWTCH, and thus, Prevent "The Great ATOMIC NIGHTMARE!" (The Saddest Story in World History!) By The Great White Bald Eagle! Book 099.}

[_] 40-054 — "The UGLY Scarred Dishonest Face of Poor Old Miserable UNCLE SAM!" (A Memorial Day Legacy!) By The Worldwide People's Revolution!® Book 054. {NOTE: This Inspired Book was also Suppressed by Amazon, who will be most Ashamed of themselves if they do not Un-suppress it during the Future: beCause it will also be Published by People of Greater Faith, who Know for a Fact that it is the TRUTH! Therefore, just be Patient. Search for Book 054B, *King James Version.*}

[_] 40-055 — "The United States of the Whole World!" (A True Global Economy for the Masses of Working People!) By The Worldwide People's Revolution!® Book 055. (This Inspired Book contains many Colored Photographs with Explanations. It is a Good Book to Publish in Foreign Nations, who are not so Blinded by their Pride, who can See the Mountain of Lies much Better at a Distance from them: beCause of not being a Part of the American Corruption.) †‡

[_] 40-056 — "The New RIGHTEOUS One-World Government!" (HOW to Establish a Righteous One-World Government without Going to WAR!) By The Worldwide People's Revolution!® Book

056. (This is a KEY Book, which everyone should Study Carefully and Prayerfully.)

[_] 40-057 — *"Those Ridiculous Contradictions within the Holy Bible!" (HOW to Read the Mutilated Bible with an Honest Open Mind!) By The Worldwide People's Revolution!®* Book 057. {NOTE: Many Professing "Christians" Falsely Claim that their so-called *"Holy Bibles"* do not Contain any Contradictions, being "the Infallible Inspired Word of the Living God," but, without the Capitalized Words, and without Explaining just WHY there are more than 200 Contradictory Versions of it! This Book Reveals how to Deal with those Biblical Problems, and come to Understand WHY God Allowed it to Happen for the Truth's Sake. Trust God: beCause, you have never Heard this Explanation before now. See also: *"C-SPAN-DEX!" (Your Filtered View of Bad Government!) By The Worldwide People's Revolution!®* Book 097.}

[_] 40-058 — **"The Divided States of United Lies!" (The so-called "United States of North America" in Disguise!) By The Worldwide People's Revolution!®** Book 058. {NOTE: This is perhaps the most Referred to Book among all of the Books by our Selected King; but, that does not Mean that it is his Best Book by any Means, which is Well Camouflaged: so that it will Survive the Test of Time, even if the others are BURNED by the Anti-Christ Followers of Satan, who are Possession Worshipers of the Worst Kind, who Seek to Justify American Lies, rather than Quickly Confess them, and thus Escape from their Self-made Prison of Propagandish Lies! Just be Perfectly Honest, and you will have no Problem with any of our Literature.}

[_] 40-059 — **"The Complete SURVEYS of our VALUES!" (SURVEYS of Religious Spiritual Political Governmental Sexual Social Moral Economical Business Labor Habitual and Miscellaneous VALUES!) By The Worldwide People's Revolution!®** Book 059. {NOTE: According to our Selected King, every Potential Leader in the World must Fill Out and File those Surveys on the Internet for everyone to Study, whereby the Best People might be Elected by those Wise People who have also Filled Out the Simplistic Surveys of their own Values, whereby they will be Qualified to VOTE. Otherwise, they will not be Qualified to Vote, which will Eliminate a LOT of Wasted Money on Election Deceptions, while at the same Time it will Educate a lot of Ignorant People, who Desperately Need to Study that Inspired Book before Voting for another Dimwitcrat, Reprobate, or Independent Jackass!}

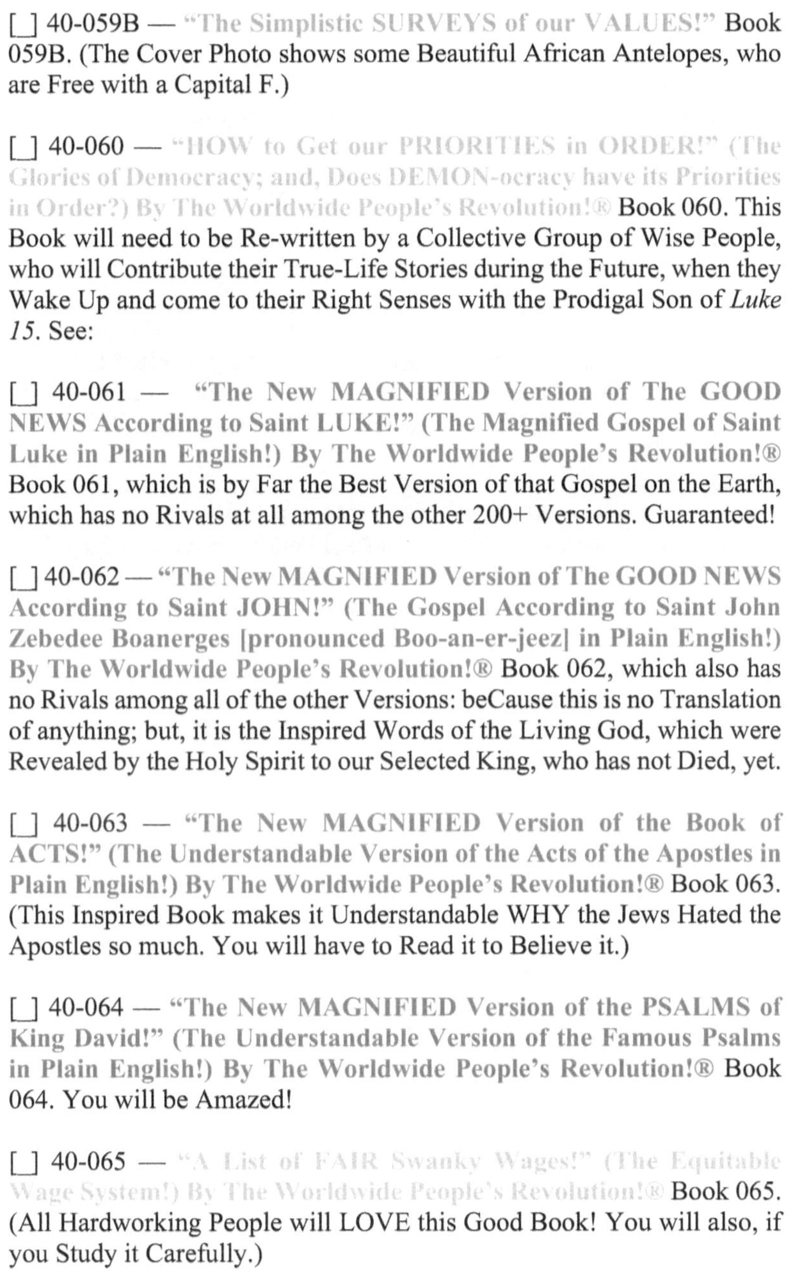

[_] 40-059B — "The Simplistic SURVEYS of our VALUES!" Book 059B. (The Cover Photo shows some Beautiful African Antelopes, who are Free with a Capital F.)

[_] 40-060 — "HOW to Get our PRIORITIES in ORDER!" (The Glories of Democracy; and, Does DEMON-ocracy have its Priorities in Order?) By The Worldwide People's Revolution!® Book 060. This Book will need to be Re-written by a Collective Group of Wise People, who will Contribute their True-Life Stories during the Future, when they Wake Up and come to their Right Senses with the Prodigal Son of *Luke 15*. See:

[_] 40-061 — "The New MAGNIFIED Version of The GOOD NEWS According to Saint LUKE!" (The Magnified Gospel of Saint Luke in Plain English!) By The Worldwide People's Revolution!® Book 061, which is by Far the Best Version of that Gospel on the Earth, which has no Rivals at all among the other 200+ Versions. Guaranteed!

[_] 40-062 — "The New MAGNIFIED Version of The GOOD NEWS According to Saint JOHN!" (The Gospel According to Saint John Zebedee Boanerges [pronounced Boo-an-er-jeez] in Plain English!) By The Worldwide People's Revolution!® Book 062, which also has no Rivals among all of the other Versions: beCause this is no Translation of anything; but, it is the Inspired Words of the Living God, which were Revealed by the Holy Spirit to our Selected King, who has not Died, yet.

[_] 40-063 — "The New MAGNIFIED Version of the Book of ACTS!" (The Understandable Version of the Acts of the Apostles in Plain English!) By The Worldwide People's Revolution!® Book 063. (This Inspired Book makes it Understandable WHY the Jews Hated the Apostles so much. You will have to Read it to Believe it.)

[_] 40-064 — "The New MAGNIFIED Version of the PSALMS of King David!" (The Understandable Version of the Famous Psalms in Plain English!) By The Worldwide People's Revolution!® Book 064. You will be Amazed!

[_] 40-065 — "A List of FAIR Swanky Wages!" (The Equitable Wage System!) By The Worldwide People's Revolution!® Book 065. (All Hardworking People will LOVE this Good Book! You will also, if you Study it Carefully.)

[_] 40-066 — "Beautiful Swanky PALACES!" (A New Concept in Living Habits — Swanky Palaces for Poor People!) By The Worldwide People's Revolution!® Book 066. (You have no Idea what a "Swanky Palace" IS, unless you have read this Unique Book, or another one that Describes those Palaces, and several of them do; but, this one has the Best Description. ENJOY!)

[_] 40-067 — "The Swanky Sword of Divine Truths!" (The Most-Powerful Weapon in the Whole Universe!) By The Worldwide People's Revolution!® Book 067. (The very Reason that our Selected King has no Rivals is beCause of the Swanky Sword of Divine Truths, which no one can Defeat by any Means. Therefore, you Need to have it on your own Side, whereby no one can Defeat your Arguments! Be Strong, be Brave, have Faith and put on the Whole Armor of GOD!)

[_] 40-068 — "Has your Life become Extremely Complicated?" (HOW to Live a SIMPLE Life!) By The Worldwide People's Revolution!® Book 068. (Many People are not even Aware of just how Complicated their Lives are, until suddenly they are ready to Commit Suicide! It is Best to Prevent all such Evil Things, and this Book tells HOW.)

[_] 40-069 — "The IDEAL Place to Live!" (HOW to Discover the Ideal Place to Live!) By The Worldwide People's Revolution!® Book 069. {NOTE: Our Selected King Searched the World over, and did not Discover any Idea Place to Live. Therefore, he Concluded that we must Make our own. Yes, we must Build those "GLORIOUS Swanky Hotels Castles and Fortresses!" (Beautiful Planned City States for WISE Intelligent Well-Educated People with Common Sense and Good Understanding!) By The Worldwide People's Revolution!® Book 019B, even if we must DRAFT "Seven Great Armies of Working Soldiers!" (HOW to Provide a Way for Everyone to WORK: so as to Eliminate Poverty, Crimes, Drug Abuses, Prisons and Unnecessary Taxes!) By The Worldwide People's Revolution!® Book 015B; and what on this Good Earth could Prove to be more Profitable than that, and without going to WAR?}

[_] 40-070 — "Our Elected King Who Speaks Out!" (It is High Time for some Sane Person to Get Control of this Insane World!) By The Worldwide People's Revolution!® Book 070. (This Inspired Book contains a Special Speech that is Addressed to both Houses of the Congress in Washington. You will Love it, O Honest Man of Greater Faith!)

[_] 40-071 — "How GAY is GOD?" (Oh, the Wonders of it all, when it ALL Hangs Out!) By The Worldwide People's Revolution!® Book 071. (Do not Judge the Book, until you have Carefully "Red" all of it. You will be Surprised by the Provable Truths within it, and Greatly Humored by the Author's Exceptionally Good Humor, who is less Gay than God, who has never had any Sexual Intercourse during his entire Life! In other Words, he is a VIRGIN!)

[_] 40-072 — "LIGHTNING STRIKES Versus Lightning Bugs and Impotent Fireflies!" (A Memorial Photo Album of some Real American Heroes!) By The Worldwide People's Revolution!® Book 072. (NOTE: This Book is Unique among all of the Books by our Selected King: beCause he did not get to Proof-read it before the Computer Crashed. It just Happened to be Saved on a Computer Chip before the Computer Crashed, and therefore it was Saved in PDF. But, the Corrections did not get made, which makes it a Special Collector's Item, which has more than 100 Colored Photos, which was what Caused the Crash.) †‡

[_] 40-073 — "The BEST of CAPITALISM!" (Corrections for: "LIGHTNING STRIKES Versus Lightning Bugs and Impotent Fireflies!") Book 073. (It is a completely new Book, except for those Corrections; and it is one of the Best Books in the World, which all Honest People will Love.)

[_] 40-074 — "LIGHTNING STRIKES Versus Lightning Bugs!" (HOW you can Become Moderately RICH, without Telling any Lies nor Selling any Trash!) By The Worldwide People's Revolution!® Book 074, which is the Perfection of all of the Lightning Striking Books, which is Recommended above all others for Mass Production: beCause it stands the Best Chance of being a Real Winner, just after this Book that you are now Reading, which has a Magnetizing Title!

[_] 40-075 — "What are the PUNISHMENTS for Dietary Sins?" (Have we Served ourselves Well at the Tables of our Lusts?) By The Worldwide People's Revolution!® Book 075. (This Book is too Controversial to be Published at this Time. Be very Patient until it is Available: beCause it is HOT!)

[_] 40-076 — "What is WRong with those CRAZY CHRISTIANS?" (A Self-Examination of the Heart of the Body of Good Government!) By The Worldwide People's Revolution!® Book 076.

121

[_] 40-077 — "The Gospel According to our Elected King!" (The Good News from the Most Modern Perspective!) By The Worldwide People's Revolution!® Book 077. (This is perhaps the Best Book that you will Discover on Amazon, which contains the Famous Sermon that Jonah gave to the Ninevites, plus a very Special Sermon by Jesus Christ, himself, which is taken from the Dead Sea Scrolls! It is simply a Marvelous Book that everyone must "Reed." ENJOY!) ‡

[_] 40-078 — "The Root Cause for almost all Evils!" (The Strange Things that People Say and Do to Get more Money!) By The Worldwide People's Revolution!® Book 078. (This Book contains many Colored Photographs with Fascinating Explanations!)

[_] 40-079 — "Orgimmick Gardening at its Best!" (HOW to Grow Delicious Satisfying Foods without a 10-Million-Dollar Investment!) By The Worldwide People's Revolution!® Book 079. (This Book also contains many Colored Photographs with Wonderful Explanations!)

[_] 40-080 — "Guaranteed Solutions!" (HOW to Solve our Local and Global Problems in the Most-Rational Manner Possible!) By The Worldwide People's Revolution!® Book 080. (See the Description on Amazon: because they Offer a ONE-MILLION-DOLLAR REWARD to anyone who can Prove our Selected King's Solutions to be WRong or Unworkable! Can you Beat that? Do you have all such Guaranteed Solutions? Does any Politician? Only our Selected King has those Provable Solutions: beCause God Blest him with them, which can be Proven in any Courtroom with Law and Order. ENJOY!)

[_] 40-081 — "Mexicans are more Intelligent than Americans!" (A Unique Challenge to all Americans and Mexicans!) By The Worldwide People's Revolution!® Book 081. {NOTE: The Remaining 275 Inspired Books by the Author of this Book may only be found in English, until we can get them Properly Translated into other Languages. Shame on you People who Killed him, who Broke his Heart with your Unbelief. May God have Mercy on your Poor Wretched Souls.} †§‡

[_] 40-081B — "¡Los Mexicanos son más Inteligentes que los Estadounidenses!" (¡Un Desafío Único para todos los Estadounidenses y Mexicanos!) By The Worldwide People's Revolution!® Book 082. {NOTA: Aquí está el primer Libro en Español, que puede no ser Perfecto; pero, es Perfectamente lo Suficientemente Bueno para Iluminar las Mentes de quien lo Estudia.}

[_] 40-082 — "The Process of Making a RIGHTEOUS KING!" (A Fascinating Autobiography of our Selected King!) By The Worldwide People's Revolution!® Book 082. {NOTE: He once had a 6,000-plus-page Autobiography, called: **"DIARRHEA of the Mind!"** which gave Details of his entire Life, since he was only 4 Years Old, when he had an Encounter with God, which has been Lost: beCause those Backup Disks became Obsolete, and were thus Trashed, along with the Obsolete Computer, which Costed 4,000-plus Dollars, along with the Hewlett-Packard Printer, which Costed another 4,000-plus Dollars, whose Antiquated Software would not Work with a Modern Computer, nor did Hewlett have an Updated Software Program for it: beCause they are Capitalist Scammers, who should be put Out of Business for Practicing Donald Trump Tactics! See: "The Nature of CAPITALISM!" (A List of the EVILS of CAPITALISM!) By The Worldwide People's Revolution!® Book 038.}

[_] 40-083 — "Was Billy Graham Greatly Deceived?" (Giving Honor to whom Honor is Due!) By The Worldwide People's Revolution!® Book 083. {NOTE: If you know a Grahamite, please Direct him or her to this Inspired Book, whereby he or she might be Converted to the Truths within it, and thus be Saved from Grahamite Perversions. Thank you in Advance. They will also Thank you for it: beCause they Suffer so Needlessly, when they should be Free, Healthy and Happy, like our Selected King, who has no Aches nor Pains, who used to Work Hard all Day long, and not be Weary, just like you can Reed in *the Book of Isaiah 40:31, NMV!*}

[_] 40-084 — "The New MAGNIFIED Version of the Book of DEUTERONOMY!" (The Understandable Version of Deuteronomy in Plain English!) Book 084. This is actually one of the Best Books within the entire Holy Bible, and also one of the Longest; but, do not allow that Fact to Deter you by any Means: beCause, "the Bigger Book is Normally a Better Book," which is True of a lot of Books, including all of the above Books: beCause it is the Nature of the Holy Spirit to get into Long-winded Sermons, you might say, which is WHY the Apostle Paul Preached until Midnight in *the Book of Acts,* until some Boy went to Sleep and Fell from a Window and Killed himself, whom the Apostle Paul Raised Up from the Dead and went on Preaching until the Dawn of the Day! And it is NOT Jewish Mythology! †§‡§§ {See: "The New MAGNIFIED Version of the Book of ACTS" for the Finest of Details, Book 063.}

[_] 40-085 — "All of the Arguments are in Favor of our Selected King, who has Zero Challengers!" (Before you Attend another Election Deception, you should Carefully Study this Inspired Book with an Honest Open Mind!) By The Worldwide People's Revolution!® Book 085.

[_] 40-086 — "Provable Truths that True Christians cannot Rightly Deny!" (A Fair Challenge for all Professing "Christians" to Meditate on with Honest Open Minds!) By The Worldwide People's Revolution!® Book 086.

[_] 40-087 — "How all Women can Get True Justice without Getting Divorced from God!" (The Unjust Case of Judge Brett Kavanaugh and Doctor Christine Blasey Ford is now Revisited by a Wise Son of King Solomon!) By The Worldwide People's Revolution!® B-087.

[_] 40-088 — "The New MAGNIFIED Version of GENESIS!" (The Enlightening Version of the Beginnings of Things!) By The Worldwide People's Revolution!® Book 088.

[_] 40-089 — "The New MAGNIFIED Version of the HOLY KORAN!" (WHY MuhamMAD went to Hell for Spiritual MURDER!) By The Worldwide People's Revolution!® Book 089. This is by Far the Best Version of the *Holy Koran,* which is Loved by all Honest Muslims, Hindus, Christians and Buddhists, Worldwide! Surprise yourself and others. Ask them what it Means? §‡

[_] 40-090 — "A New Jerusalem in the Great State of Flexible Texas!" (HOW to make Good Use of the Mississippi River!) By The Worldwide People's Revolution!® Book 090. This Book contains many Fascinating Photos of God's Handiwork. ENJOY!

[_] 40-091 — "What is The GREATEST SIN?" (And it is NOT Blasphemy Against the Holy Spirit!) By The Worldwide People's Revolution!® Book 091.

[_] 40-092 — "HOW to Make America (and all other Nations) Really GREAT Without Telling any LIES!" (The Founding Fathers would have Loved it!) By The Worldwide People's Revolution!® Book 092.

[_] 40-093 — "HOW Righteousness can Overcome Wickedness!" (The Triumph of the Soul who Knows God!) By The Enlightened Professor of Common Sense! Book 093. {Notice how the Calves in the

Cover Photo Segregated themselves by their Colors, from Left to Right. God Guided them. ‡}

[_] 40-094 — "Justifications for MAGNIFICATIONS!" (The Problem with Understanding a Complicated Contradictory Mutilated Unholy Bible!) Or: (The Problem with Inventing Lies that are too BIG to DIE!) By The Worldwide People's Revolution!® Book 094.

[_] 40-095 — "HOW to IDENTIFY God's Elected Ones!" (Are YOU one of the Elect?) By The Worldwide People's Revolution!® Book 095.

[_] 40-096 — "GOVERNMENT Versus Independence!" (How Much CONTROL Should a Government Have?") By The Worldwide People's Revolution!® Book 096.

[_] 40-097 — "C-SPAN-DEX!" (Your Filtered View of Bad Government!) By The Worldwide People's Revolution!® Book 097.

[_] 40-098 — "Profitable Swanky MULCHING ROCKS!" (30 Advantages for Using Swanky Mulching Rocks in an All-Mineral Organic Garden!) By The Worldwide People's Revolution!® Book 098. {Just Think, the School of Fools never Mentioned them, nor did the False Government, nor any of the False Churches: beCause they are Uneducated and Foolish.}

[_] 40-099 — "The Great ATOMIC NIGHTMARE!" (The Saddest Story in World History!) By The Great White Bald Eagle! Book 099. {NOTE: Let us Hope and Pray that no one ever has to Write this Book; but, if they Do, it should Spook the Devil Out of you!}

[_] 40-100 — "Our Selected King SPEAKS OUT!" (It is High Time for some Sane Person to get Total Control of this Insane World!) By The Worldwide People's Revolution!® Book 100!

[_] 40-101 — "What will you Do when the Rain STOPS?" (God's Last Resort to Save Mankind from his MADNESS!) By The Worldwide People's Revolution!® Book 101!

[_] 40-102 — "Beautiful Swanky Stone Dome Home COMPLEXES!" (HOW to Build SECURE Tax-proof, Insurance-proof, Self-air-conditioned, Paint-proof, Rot-proof, Termite-proof, Mouse-proof, Fireproof, Tornado-proof, Hurricane-proof, Thief-proof, and BOMB-PROOF Houses!) By The Worldwide People's Revolution!® Book 102.

[_] 40-103 — "Royal Swanky Buffets!" (The Best Feasts in the Whole World!) By The Worldwide People's Revolution!® Book 103.

[_] 40-104 — "101 Good Reasons and Great Advantages for Establishing a Righteous One-World Government!" (Government By the People, Of the People, and For the People!) By The Worldwide People's Revolution!® Book 104. This Book Suggests thousands of Good Reasons and Great Advantages. But, of course, you have to be Able to THINK, which seems to be something that Wicked Politicians cannot Do, or Refuse to Do; and neither can most Preachers and Teachers Do it. Therefore, this Inspired Book will Help them to Think and Remember.

[_] 40-105 — "The New MAGNIFIED Version of the Book of REVELATION!" (The Understandable Version of the Most-Controversial Book in the Whole World!) By The Worldwide People's Revolution!® Book 105. This Proverbial "Bombshell" will be Published just before the Second Coming of Jesus Christ! Get your Seatbelts Fastened! Be Prepared for Radical Changes!

[_] 40-106 — "The Naked Glory of Beautiful Mankind!" (1,000 Pages of Sheer Artistic BEAUTY!) By The Worldwide People's Revolution!® Book 106. (See Book 014B-02-09-T for the Explanation.)

[_] 40-107 — "The Beautiful Faces of Holy Men!" (The very Best that God has to Offer!) By The Worldwide People's Revolution!® Book 107.

[_] 40-108 — "The Worldwide People's Revolution!" (A Comprehensive Plan for Obtaining Worldwide Law, Order, Obedience, Peace and True Prosperity!) By The Worldwide People's Revolution!® Book 108.

[_] 40-109 — "VOTE for The GOAT!" (The New Political Party that has Guaranteed Solutions for our Massive Problems!) By The Worldwide People's Revolution!® Book 109.

[_] 40-110 — "IMPORTANT THINGS that Should Have Been Written in the Holy Bible!" (A Special Challenge to all Professing Christians, Jews, Hindus, Muslims and Atheists!) **By** The Irreverent Penname Scumbag! Book 110.

[_] 40-111 — "Hosts of HOAXES Live In Under Around and Over the Little White OUTHOUSE!" (WHY Spiritually-Blind Cowardly-Americans are Hunkering Down in their Empty Root Cellars!) **By** The Irreverent Penname Oversight! Book 111.

[_] 40-112 — "Should Wives Obey their Husbands?" (OR, Should Husbands OBEY their Wives?) By The Irreverent Penname Mockingbird! Book 112.

[_] 40-113 — "Modern Deceived SLAVES!" (10 Simple Steps for Liberating ALL Modern Slaves, Worldwide, Including Yourself!) **By** Liberty and Justice for ALL! Book 113.

[_] 40-114 — "Are you a Jobless Graduate of the School of Fools?" (How to Obtain a Good Education without Robbing the Bank, Selling any Trash, nor Telling any Lies!) **By** The Professor Wordcraft Enlightenment! Book 114.

[_] 40-115 — "Beautiful Swanky FASTING SANITARIUMS!" (HOW to Learn Good Self-Discipline!) **By** The Worldwide People's Revolution!® Book 115.

[_] 40-116 — "Swanky Institutions for Compassionate Corrections!" (How to Correct even the Most-Stubborn Bullies!) **By** The Biggest Bully of All Bullies! Book 116.

[_] 40-117 — "What is True PROGRESS???" (Are we Making any True Progress, at all?) By The Worldwide People's Revolution!® Book 117.

[_] 40-118 — "Is America a White Nation with a Black Heart?" (How to Separate Truth from Fiction!) **By** The Good Pastor of Uncommon Sense! Book 118.

[_] 40-119 — "Which Church is the Right Church?" (Can all Churches be Correct?) **By** The Good Pastor of Uncommon Sense! Book 119.

[_] 40-120 — "Do People Go to Heaven when they Die?" (The Unbelievable Truth about Life and Death!) **By The Good Pastor of Uncommon Sense!** Book 120.

[_] 40-121 — "The Hopeless Church of Little Faith!" (The Unholy Church of Graceful Sinners, who are Mostly just Liars and Hypocrites!) **By The Good Pastor of Uncommon Sense!** Book 121.

{NOTE: That List of Available Books will be Updated, Periodically, if we do not get Killed by some Thugs, who Work for those Lying Conniving Edomites!}